D0591231
CHERISHED
LIBRARY

Schools Library Service
556736

England
A Very Peculiar History™

Volume 1

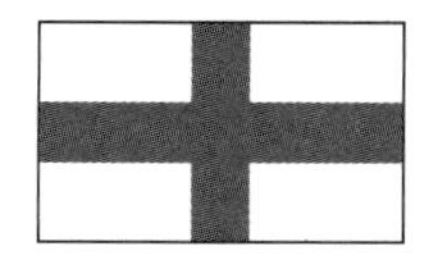

'This happy breed of men, this little world,
This precious stone set in the silver sea.'

William Shakespeare, *Richard II*

For Jill, true north to my soft south

DA

Editor: Stephen Haynes
Editorial assistants: Rob Walker, Mark Williams

Published in Great Britain in MMXIII by
Book House, an imprint of
The Salariya Book Company Ltd
25 Marlborough Place, Brighton BN1 1UB
www.salariya.com
www.book-house.co.uk

HB ISBN-13: 978-1-908973-37-5 vol. 1
978-1-908973-38-2 vol. 2
978-1-908973-39-9 vol. 3
978-1-908973-41-2 boxed set

1 3 5 7 9 8 6 4 2
A CIP catalogue record for this book is available from the British Library.
Printed and bound in Dubai.

England
A Very Peculiar History™

Volume 1

From Ancient Times to Agincourt

By
David Arscott

Created and designed by
David Salariya

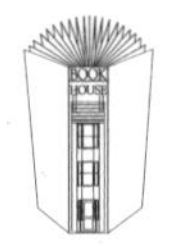

'Remember that you are an Englishman,
and have consequently won first place
in the lottery of life.'
Cecil Rhodes

'Let not England forget her precedence
of teaching nations how to live.'
John Milton

'Every Englishman is convinced of one thing,
viz; that to be an Englishman is to belong to
the most exclusive club there is.'
Ogden Nash

'It is a mark of self confidence: the English
have not spent a great deal of time defining
themselves because they haven't needed to.'
Jeremy Paxman

'You never find an Englishman among the
under-dogs – except in England, of course.'
Evelyn Waugh

Contents

So, who do the English think they are?

A MONGREL RACE

Just who *are* the English, and what right have they to gloat about themselves with the shocking nose-in-the-air disdain for other nations that we've already encountered in these pages?

These are difficult questions to answer, but we shall enthusiastically buckle down to the task throughout these three volumes. History may have uncomfortable lessons to teach (gung-ho nationalists should beware the thorns that cluster around our sweet English rose), but it bestows a sense of identity, too.

What no English man or woman can lay claim to is 'pure' blood, in the sense of descending in an unbroken line from some ideal forebear, whether Saxon, Viking or anything else. Thanks to millennia of wandering, settling and intermarrying, we are a decidedly mongrel race – and none the worse for that.

Our unfolding story will tell of early hunter-gatherers and the first farmers; of Roman occupation eventually giving way to the often brutal thrusts of land-hungry Anglo-Saxons; of Viking incursions and the 1066 conquest by their cousins, the Normans; and of later incomers from all parts of the globe in the wake of the Industrial Revolution and the spread of the Empire until, especially in its cities, England becomes a vibrant multicultural society.

Whereas we once sought to plot the restless movements of prehistoric people through the artefacts they left behind or the words they passed on, today we can cull additional evidence from a simple swab in the mouth. In order to trace our origins, geneticists work with mitochondrial DNA, inherited by all of us from our mothers, and with the Y chromosome, passed directly to men from their fathers. The more feisty of these experts argue ferociously about the details, but here are a few of their basic findings as they relate to white English men and women:

- **The nation's genetic make-up remains essentially what it was in prehistoric times.**
- **Although the Anglo-Saxons had a profound influence on our island history, their contribution to the gene pool is only about 20 per cent in East Anglia, where they make their strongest showing.**
- **The Viking bloodline is, unsurprisingly, much more significant in central, northern and eastern parts of the country – the Danelaw.**
- **The Normans, who suppressed the Saxon peasantry without mingling much with them, have bestowed a measly 2 per cent of our genes.**

A further shock-horror discovery has been that the neighbouring Scots and Welsh share many of their genes with the English – which tells us that the search for national identity has to be found in culture rather than genetics.

Continent cut off

A Fleet Street headline is once supposed to have announced 'Fog in the Channel – Europe cut off.' That may be apocryphal, but possibly not: the fact that rising sea levels separated southern England from the Continent some 8,000 years ago has clearly played a major role in shaping our national psyche. We have an island mentality.

You'll encounter many aspects of this in the pages that follow, from the creation of the first navy under King Alfred, through the exploits of enterprising Elizabethan seafarers such as Drake and Raleigh to the relentless quest for overseas adventure and conquest which by the 1920s saw a quarter of the world's map coloured pink, and an incredible one fifth of its population under the sway of the British Empire.

This go-it-alone attitude is sometimes interpreted by other nations as overweening arrogance, but no matter: we shall be following Oliver Cromwell's reported advice to his portrait painter to create an honest picture, 'warts and all'. Many heroes and villains will pass before our eyes, and you must use your own judgement to separate the sheep from the goats. How, for example, would you rate the following?

- **Richard the Lionheart:** A dashing figure at the head of a noble Crusade – bent on pillaging lands to which he had no right.
- **Oliver Cromwell:** A firebrand against the tyranny of the Crown – whose 'warts' included becoming a virtual dictator himself.
- **Clive of India:** The British officer and Tory MP secured India and its wealth for the Crown – but his East India Company was corrupt, and (although Parliament exonerated him) he committed suicide in disgrace.
- **Field Marshal Sir Douglas Haig:** The man who won vital victories against Germany during the First World War, and then helped establish the Royal British Legion – but was later vilified for his role in the mass carnage of the Somme.
- **Margaret Thatcher:** The 'Iron Lady' boasted of taming the trade unions after coming to power in 1979 – but her free-market policies divided the nation.

'Cry God for Harry, England and St George!'

The stirring battle cry that Shakespeare attributes to Henry V at Agincourt honours a saint who had nothing whatsoever to do with England, but whose supposed exploits and martyr's death had long made him an icon across the Christian world.

George is thought to have been born into a noble family around AD 275 in Cappadocia (modern Turkey), and to have served in Diocletian's imperial guard. He never really fought a dragon, of course, but he apparently displayed an equal bravery in opposing the emperor's edict against Christianity and refusing to worship the Roman gods. For this he was horribly tortured (three times lacerated on a wheel of swords before being resuscitated) and then decapitated.

St George was officially recognised as the patron saint of England by the late 14th century, but his emblem of a red cross on a white ground had already been adopted by crusaders, who reported his miraculous appearance to them before their battles against 'the infidel' in the Holy Land.

How the other half lived

History is not just kings and queens. These volumes certainly record the colourful, often outrageous, exploits of those at the top of the pile (and there's a handy checklist on pages 177–178), but we're every bit as interested in the lives of ordinary men, women and children. How did the likes of us rub along through the ages – how much did they earn, what did they eat and drink, how did they use what little leisure time they had, how long did they live?

What we select from this rich tapestry in order to create a sense of national identity is a matter of personal choice. Some will pick out threads which promote a developing story of English influence in the world. Others, happy to stay at home, will rather favour an 'everyman' celebration of growing liberty and spreading democracy.

Few, it's safe to say, will look for inspiration to the very earliest inhabitants of this little patch of earth, but it's with them that we start – small bands of hunter-gatherers scratching a scant living from a hostile environment...

Henry the *Split* and *all* that

For the genuine potted history of England you need go no further than these pages, but the ideal companion is a work which was first serialised in *Punch* magazine and then published in book form in 1930. It has never been out of print since.

In *1066 and All That*, W. C. Sellar and R. J. Yeatman have great fun guying the worthy school textbooks of the period. Their subtitle gives the flavour: 'A Memorable History of England, comprising all the parts you can remember, including 103 Good Things, 5 Bad Kings and 2 Genuine Dates.'

We read about the Split King, Henry IV (parts 1 and 2), the Disillusion of the Monasteries and the Industrial Revelation, and we're invited to take five nonsense test papers, complete with daft instructions.

Prime Minister Gladstone, we learn, failed his own test, having 'spent his declining years trying to guess the answer to the Irish Question; unfortunately, whenever he was getting warm, the Irish secretly changed the Question'.

The book begins with the Romans and ends with the First World War, by which time America has become Top Nation – and history has therefore come to a full stop.

As she is spoke

The spread of empire has given English a major place among world languages:

- There are some 380 million native speakers, neck-and-neck with Spanish and outstripped only by Mandarin.
- A further 250 million people use it as their second language.
- In all, around 1.8 billion people handle it with some degree of competence.

Here are just a few of the countries around the world which use English as an official language:

Antigua and Barbuda
Barbados
Belize
Botswana
Cameroon
Canada
Dominica
Eritrea
Ethiopia
Fiji
The Gambia
Grenada
Guyana
India
Ireland
Jamaica
Kenya
Lesotho
Liberia
Malawi
Malta
Mauritius
Namibia
Nauru
New Zealand
Nigeria
Pakistan
Papua New Guinea
Philippines
Rwanda
St Kitts and Nevis
St Lucia
Samoa
Seychelles
Sierra Leone
Singapore
Sudan
Tanzania
Tonga
Trinidad and Tobago
Uganda
Vanuatu
Zambia
Zimbabwe

Ten things to thank the *early* English *for*

1. **Stonehenge** It's said that they brought more than 80 heavy bluestones some 150 miles (240 km) from Wales, but we can only guess why they went to the trouble. Was their massive stone circle a burial site, a temple, a healing centre or an astronomical clock?

2. **The Navy** Every maritime nation expects to have one these days, but King Alfred set the precedent by organising a 9th-century fleet to keep the marauding Vikings at bay.

3. **The English language** Our incredibly rich tongue has an Anglo-Saxon base, with accretions of Norman French and a teeming vocabulary adapted from nations around the world. Now it's the universal lingua franca.

4. **Saxon churches** Although the Normans rebuilt or expanded many of those they found, many simple pre-Conquest churches survive – some (such as Escomb in County Durham) dating from the 7th century.

5. **The Domesday Book** It was hated at the time, because this record of land ownership was used by the new Norman masters to tax the people. For modern historians, though, it's a unique guide to England just after the Conquest.

6. **Norman cathedrals and minsters** They started no fewer than 15 of these soon after 1066, and they kept adapting and expanding them over the years. The one at Old Sarum was replaced by a new pile at nearby Salisbury, but all the others can still be visited – from Durham in the north to Chichester in the south; from Norwich in the east to Gloucester in the west.

7. **Trial by jury** The right to be judged by our fellow men and women, rather than representatives of a power elite, is central to our legal system. Henry II created the templates of our current jury and Common Law systems in the late 12th century.

8. **Magna Carta** True democracy was still a long way off, but at Runnymede in 1215 King John became the first monarch forced to make concessions to his subjects – the restless barons.

9. **Geoffrey Chaucer** 'The father of English literature' wrote *The Canterbury Tales* and other works in flexible Middle English, and was the very first occupant of Poets' Corner in Westminster Abbey.

10. **Football** Much later we would codify the sport, but it was already popular in 1170. A visitor to London noted that 'after dinner all the youths of the city' went out to play it, and that each trade had its own team.

Putting early England on the map

1. Stonehenge, c. 3100 BC: neolithic World Heritage Site
2. Silchester: Iron Age town later developed by the Romans
3. Fishbourne Roman Palace: thought to be the home of the Roman client king Togidubnus (or Cogidubnus)
4. Hadrian's Wall, AD 128: built to secure the northern border of Roman England
5. Antonine Wall: a later, less permanent defence between the Forth and the Clyde
6. Aquae Sulis (Bath): Roman leisure and religious centre based on Britain's only hot spring
7. Sutton Hoo: 7th-century Saxon ship burial
8. Lindisfarne (Holy Island): monastery sacked by Vikings in AD 793
9. Jorvik (York): the major Viking settlement in England
10. Winchester: King Alfred's Wessex capital
11. Westminster Abbey, London: begun by Edward the Confessor, consecrated 1065
12. Battle of Stamford Bridge, 1066: won by King Harold
13. Battle of Hastings, 1066: Harold defeated by William of Normandy, 'the Conqueror'
14. 'Marcher' castles: built by the Normans to control the Welsh border country
15. Fountains Abbey: wealthy Cistercian abbey that flourished in the 13th century
16. Laxton, Nottinghamshire: relic of medieval open-field system

N
W
E
S
SCOTLAND
ENGLAND
WALES
5
8
4
12
15
9
16
14
7
6
2
11
1
10
3
13

An early resident of England gets to grips with Stone Age technology

CHAPTER ONE

BEFORE THEY WROTE IT DOWN

As the weather warmed, so the people moved in. Welcome to our hardy nomadic ancestors, who some 15,000 years ago took advantage of the retreating ice cap to forage for fruit and snare wild animals, birds and fish in a landscape slowly returning to life. Earlier kinds of humans had been here before and had fled the big freeze-up, but this new wave of Stone Age immigrants – originally from the Middle East, and arriving via the Balkans – was here to stay. The story of England had begun.

Prehistoric England

The term 'prehistory' refers to the period before we have any written records. In our case that extends to the Iron Age, although Roman writers such as Tacitus did give some accounts of the tribes they were about to invade.

The early inhabitants knew nothing of national boundaries and the Romans regarded Britain as a single entity, so the words 'England' and 'English' in this chapter simply mean the area covered by the country today and the people who then lived in it.

Here's your handy prehistoric timeline (all dates approximate):

145 million years ago: Cretaceous period; dinosaurs flourish.

65 million years ago: Dinosaurs become extinct.

2.6 million years ago: Palaeolithic period.

125,000 years ago: Last Ice Age begins.

6000 BC: Mesolithic period; rising sea-level separates England from the Continent; hunter-gatherers active.

4500 BC: Neolithic period; first farmers.

2100–700 BC: Bronze Age.

700 BC: Iron Age.

In good seasons their diet of berries and meat was healthy, but in leaner times these hunter-gatherers faced long journeys and dangerous forays with simple flint weapons into woods harbouring bears, wild boar, wolves and lynxes.

Their numbers were tiny. It's been estimated that there were little more than a thousand humans here in 9000 BC, and that even five millennia later you would have found only about 100,000 men, women and children scattered through the whole island.

A home of their own

By this time some of them were beginning to settle down. They'd discovered farming. In the wooded lowland areas they employed a 'slash and burn' technique to create clearings where they grew basic cereal crops. They tended early forms of cattle, sheep, goats and the domestic pig, bred from wild boar. (Their tame dogs had, similarly, once been wolves.)

As their farms clustered together, so villages and, eventually, small towns began to sprout.

This concentration of settlements has given archaeologists plenty of evidence to dig up, and what emerges is a steady growth in technical sophistication.

- Tools and weapons were made by 'knapping' flints to create an edge, using a tough hammer stone or a softer bone or antler. As the centuries passed, knives and axes were given a more durable blade by using abrasive sand mixed with water to create a polished finish.

- Pottery was produced by the first farmers. The technology required the control of high temperatures, and so was a landmark advance.

- Coppicing – cutting trees back to their stools on a regular basis – produced slender shoots used to weave fences and hurdles.

- Carpentry was another neolithic 'first', trees being felled to provide the structural timbers for sturdy buildings – typically with thatched roofs and walls of woven rods weatherproofed with clay, straw and dung.

Most of these growing settlements show no signs of being defended (were these unusually peaceful times?), but there's a striking exception in Cornwall. Here you'll find the so-called 'tor enclosures', the most famous being Carn Brea, with massive granite blocks manoeuvred to infill natural rock outcrops and to seal off hilltops.

It goes without saying that historians argue endlessly about what was going on here (whether people lived continously inside these ramparts, for instance, or used them as ceremonial centres), but they all agree on the phenomenal ingenuity of a 'primitive' society which somehow organised and carried out such a large-scale enterprise – which brings us to the daddy of all prehistoric monuments...

Making tracks

The counting of tree rings (dendrochronology) has yielded an exact date for the earliest known wooden trackway in Europe – on the Somerset Levels in the west of England.

The so-called Sweet Track is a wooden footpath raised above marshy ground on crossed-timber supports. It first carried neolithic locals from high ground to an island across the bog between the winter of 3807 BC and the following spring.

Stonehenge

Neolithic henges – circular ditches with external banks enclosing an area of posts or standing stones – are unique to Britain and Ireland. At Avebury, at the west end of the Berkshire Downs, the outermost of three stone circles is the largest in Britain, with a circumference of 1,088 ft (332 m), and there were originally 98 sarsen standing stones inside.

Famous though it is, Avebury yields first place in the pantheon to Stonehenge, 17 miles (27 km) south on Salisbury Plain. With its 'goal post' lintels above heavy standing stones, it justifies that overused word *iconic*. The ditch and bank dates from around 3100 BC, and carbon dating suggests that the first stones were put up some 500 years later. Changes (new stones, new arrangements) were made to it until as late as 1600 BC.

It's been a known 'fact' for many years that Stonehenge's bluestones were brought all the way from the Preseli Hills in Wales, but a recent theory is that the stones were deposited close to the area by a glacier.

Tess's farewell

Druids welcome in the summer solstice at Stonehenge every year, and the brooding outline of its pagan presence against the sky made it a fitting place for Thomas Hardy to 'sacrifice' poor Tess in his novel *Tess of the d'Urbervilles*. Pursued by the police for a murder every reader sympathises with, she arrives at the site at night with the man she loves, Angel Clare:

> 'What monstrous place is this?'
> 'It hums,' said she. 'Hearken!'
> He listened. The wind playing upon the edifice, produced a booming tune, like the note of some gigantic one-stringed harp.

Tess lies down on one of the slabs, which Clare describes as an altar. Later, the police come to take her away – and in the final chapter she hangs.

Stonehenge lies at the centre of a large complex of Neolithic and Bronze Age monuments – including the henges at Avebury and Marden, the artificial chalk pile of Silbury Hill and several hundred burial mounds – but we know very little about the people who used it or why so many were buried here.

What it was 'for' has preoccupied both historians and fantasists throughout the ages. Perhaps it was:

- **a monument to Britons killed by the Saxons. Geoffrey of Monmouth, in his 12th-century *Historia Regum Britanniae* (*History of the Kings of Britain*), suggested it was created for this purpose by the wizard Merlin – so setting many an Arthurian hare running ever after.**

- **a temple, where large numbers of worshippers would gather to honour the ancient gods or perhaps the sun and the moon.**

- **a place of the dead. One expert has suggested that the area around Durrington Walls henge 1.9 miles (3 km) away was a place of the living, and that a journey along the Avon to Stonehenge was part of a ritual passage from life to death, to celebrate past ancestors and the recently deceased.**

- a prehistoric Lourdes. People came to Stonehenge for its healing qualities – hence the burials of such incomers as a metalworker from the foothills of Alpine Germany, a teenage boy from the Mediterranean and the 'Boscombe Bowmen' from Wales or Brittany.

- an observatory. The stones were aligned to mark sunrise at the summer solstice and the equinoxes.

The Battle of Seahenge

Some henges were made of timber, and the discovery of one on a Norfolk beach in 1998 caused a major row. Seahenge, at Holme-next-the-Sea, comprised 55 split oak trunks in a circle. Tests showed that all the trees had been felled in the spring or summer of 2049 BC.

The locals wanted it left as a tourist attraction; the Norfolk Wildlife Trust was alarmed by the prospect of visitors tramping over a nature reserve; archaeologists wanted to remove it for preservation; and neopagans claimed that tampering with it would be an insult to the beliefs of its original builders.

It was the archaeologists who won the day, and Seahenge can now be seen at the Lynn Museum in King's Lynn.

How they were buried in prehistoric times

Funeral practices change over time, and this is nowhere more evident than in the varying styles of burial mounds, or *tumuli*, over the long span covered by prehistoric England.

Because they were so prominent in the landscape, they were ransacked by robbers and often excavated inexpertly by Victorian amateur archaelogists.

- From around 4000 BC people buried their dead in communal 'long barrows' – chambered tombs made of large stones or stout timbers and covered with earth, chalk or stones.
- By 3000 BC 'passage graves' had developed. These had a central 'hall', with side chambers reached by long, low passages.
- By 1500 BC the communal idea had given way to single burials in 'round barrows'. These often included treasured possessions, the 'grave goods' including daggers and valuable objects of gold and amber. Variations on this theme included the 'bell barrow', which had a surrounding ditch and sometimes a low bank beyond it.
- After 1500 BC, cremation in cemeteries became the fashion, with or without barrows.

Meet the Beaker folk

It's not much of a compliment to be named after a drinking cup, but archaeologists have named a whole subculture the 'Beaker Folk' after the highly decorated, flat-bottomed pottery discovered at countless sites in western Europe from around 2000 BC. An old theory was that a wave of incomers brought the necessary techniques to England with them, but (as we've seen) geneticists have poured cold water on that idea, and it seems that it was the know-how and the fashion that spread, rather than the people.

The beakers were used not only for drink and food, but as funerary urns and – please step through to the Bronze Age – 'reduction pots' for the smelting of copper ores. New furnace technology, providing higher temperatures fanned by hide bellows, ushered in what must have seemed a wonderful new world of gold, copper and bronze metalwork.

While flint tools and weapons continued to be chipped alongside them, now there were tough spearheads, axes and knives fashioned in copper and bronze – an alloy of 90 per cent copper to 10 per cent tin. Gold provided precious ornaments and jewellery.

Digging Deep

Tin was exploited in Cornwall and west Devon, but at this time supplies were found on or near the surface; the sinking of deep mines would await a later age.

In the chalk districts of southern England, on the other hand, flint mines were sunk to a depth of 50 ft (15 m), with radiating galleries from each shaft. At Grime's Graves in Norfolk – where you can descend the only surviving example – it's estimated that 2,000 tonnes of chalk were removed from each shaft, requiring the labour of twenty men armed with picks of red-deer antler over a period of five months.

The work must have been hard and dangerous. An excavation at Cissbury in Sussex discovered the skeleton of a 20-year-old woman in one of the galleries, a torch still held in her bony grasp.

On the prehistoric map

You'll find many clues to the relics of ancient England on a detailed Ordnance Survey map:

- **Tumulus.** A long, round or other burial mound (see page 30). They're often clustered together; *tumuli* is the plural.
- **Flint mines.** Always plural, because many shafts were sunk in the same area. The telltale sign today is dimpling in the turf.
- **Enclosure.** One or more Bronze Age round houses set within circular ditches and banks.
- **Causewayed enclosure.** Here's a mystery. These enclosures are large circular areas set within ditches which have numerous crossing points, and the best guess – since the ditches often contain 'offerings' such as human and animal bones, pottery and unused stone axes – is that they had a ceremonial function.
- **Cross dyke.** Another head-scratcher. These were ditches between parallel banks running from one hilltop spur to another, and so linking the heads of valleys. Droveways? Substantial farm boundaries? Nobody knows.
- **Field system.** Ancient fields often appear as terracing – 'lynchets' – where soil has slipped from higher fields to settle above those below.

Men of iron

When archaeologists from nearby Reading University recovered an olive stone from a well at Silchester in 2012, they heralded it as the ultimate proof of their long-held thesis – that the Iron Age inhabitants enjoyed a lifestyle that wouldn't have disgraced a well-to-do citizen of Rome.

The Greek geographer Strabo, writing in the 1st century AD, gave an idea of the trade between Britain and the Continent. Our exports included precious metals, corn, cattle, hides, hunting-dogs and slaves, while we bought in fabrics, wine and olive oil.

Buried treasure

The idea that early Bronze Age burials with rich grave goods were exclusive to the Stonehenge area was exploded by a 1993 excavation in Leicestershire. What came to be known as the Lockington Gold Hoard comprised parts of two pottery vessels, two decorated gold armlets and a copper dagger thought to have come from Brittany.

It was clear even from this simple list that the better-off English were no woad-painted savages, but people with a taste for the good life.

The excavations at Silchester, involving hundreds of amateur and professional volunteers for more than a decade, have put flesh on these bare bones:

- These pre-Roman English grew dill, marigold, mint, coriander, fennel and curry plants in their herb gardens, and they further flavoured their food with onion, celery and poppy seeds.
- Their diet included shellfish as well as cows, pigs, sheep, domesticated geese and chickens.
- From their fields and orchards they harvested wheat, apples, cherries, blackberries and plums – plus olives.
- At mealtimes they ate off plates and washed down their food with wine.
- Their imports included luxury drinking glasses and pottery, gold from Ireland and bronze jewellery from the Continent.

Silchester is thought to have been founded around 50 BC by Commius, a leader of the Atrebates tribe from what is now France, who had been a friend of Julius Caesar but was forced to flee Gaul for his life after taking part in a failed rebellion against him.

At Silchester – Calleva Atrebatum in Latin – his people lived in large houses, built alongside gravel roads and aligned with the sunrises and sunsets of the summer and winter solstices. They exported metalwork and (as Strabo reported) corn, hunting dogs and slaves. They also – animal lovers please look away – seem to have used the skins of puppies to make quality cloaks.

Well-to-do

From Silchester and other investigations we have a picture of a settled and prosperous population, albeit one where various tribes were regularly at war with one another.

- Much of lowland England had been cleared for the plough, and the population had grown to more than a million.
- As the name of the age implies, new techniques allowed a wide use of iron for tools and weapons.
- A rudimentary cash economy had developed, and from around 75 BC we can trace the movement of different groups by the coins they left behind.
- Concentric earthen ramparts topped by timber palisades defended impressive hill forts, chiefly in the south and west, where there were hundreds – notably Maiden Castle in Dorset, Cadbury Castle in Somerset and Danebury, Hampshire. Experts argue about whether they were inhabited most of the time, and whether their prime use was ceremonial rather than military.

These contented folk spoke a form of the Celtic language and their lifestyle, too, was similar to that of the Celts across the water in Gaul: Gallo-Belgic coins have been found in the region dating from 100 BC onwards. Commius is a prime example of a Celt who had crossed over from the Continent in recent times.

It was inevitable, then, that the Romans, having conquered Transalpine Gaul in 124 BC, would eventually turn their attention to an island which they found exotic, because largely unknown. It was fabled for its tin, and therefore promised riches, but as it was believed to be populated by tribes of brave 'barbarians', invading it would also be a feather in any conqueror's cap.

Julius Caesar was the first to try it, although it's not clear how ambitious his two expeditions were. He came in 55 BC and again the following year, on both occasions landing not far from modern-day Dover in Kent. In his *Commentarii de Bello Gallico* (*Account of the Gallic War* – which is, of course, self-serving), he writes about a mist-shrouded, 'triangular' island, about the natives' use of chariots in warfare (evidently new to him) and about the ingenuity of his victories.

His second incursion took him across the Thames and into the territory of the British leader Cassivellaunus, who had not long since seized the territory of his neighbours, the Trinovantes. Caesar defeated him, set up a friendly ruler in his place, took hostages home with him and demanded an annual tribute to Rome.

With hindsight these forays and skirmishes have the flavour of a soldier's summer holiday, and Caesar, who would declare himself 'dictator' in Rome in 49 BC, soon had more pressing matters to deal with. It would be almost a century before the legions returned – but this time they meant business.

Marcus and Sextus look forward to the end of their tour of duty in Britannia

Chapter Two

ROMAN WAYS

The moment he heard that the legionaries were marching towards his Sussex base, the local tribal leader Togidubnus knew what he was going to do – welcome them with open arms.

Emperor Claudius's invasion of AD 43, launched in Kent as Caesar's landings had been, depended on succouring friends as well as defeating enemies. Those friends knew that they stood to gain influence, handsome financial rewards and even new territory.

fabulous fishbourne

In 1960, workers digging a trench across a field in the village of Fishbourne, on an inlet of Chichester Harbour, came across the remains of a building similar in size to Nero's Golden House in Rome and mirroring the plan of the emperor Domitian's palace, the Domus Flavia, built in AD 92 on the Palatine Hill in Rome.

Archaeologists dated the Fishbourne 'palace' to the 1st century AD. What they were uncovering was surely the resplendent home of the Romans' favourite client king, Togidubnus.

The southern part had already been covered with housing, but today the excavated northern section is on display to the public, revealing how a wealthy Romano-Briton expected to live:

Mosaics. The celebrated 'Boy on a Dolphin' is but one of many outstanding floor coverings.

Central heating. Underfloor 'hypocausts' brought warm air to all the important rooms.

Fittings and furnishings. Elaborately painted walls; delicate mouldings of white Turkish and blue Purbeck marble; bronze and marble works of art – no expense spared.

Gardens. The formal gardens at the centre of the villa have been recreated, with plantings of espalier apple trees, box, lily and acanthus.

This wasn't a matter of cowardice or treachery. The Romans regarded Britain as an entity, but this was far from being a nation state and the local chieftains saw no further than their tribal borders. Some British tribes, such as Togidubnus's Atrebates, had long been friendly with the great power across the water and so welcomed its support against their enemies.

Togidubnus and his brothers are thought to have been educated in Rome, and his predecessor Verica – threatened by the growing power of the Catuvellauni – had fled there to ask for help. Now here it was in all its glistening armour.

The rewards for Togidubnus included control over some other tribes as ruler of a newly created enclave extraterritorial to the rest of the province. He was *rex et legatus Augusti in Britannia* – both a client king and a Roman official – and his people were dubbed the Regnenses (the people of the native kingdom). The sumptuous palace at Fishbourne, the largest known Roman residence north of the Alps, was almost certainly his.

The compliance of the trusted Togidubnus allowed Vespasian's Second Augustan Legion to establish a military base at what soon became the trading centre of Noviomagus (modern Chichester) – a vital launching pad for an assault on hostile tribes to the west.

Cussed Caratacus

While some local chieftains welcomed the Romans and some surrendered to avoid what would have been inevitable defeat, others put up a gutsy resistance – none more so than Caratacus of the Catuvellauni, whose guerilla tactics harrassed the invaders for some nine years before his final defeat and capture.

It was his pestering of Verica's Atrebates tribe which had triggered the invasion in the first place, and he led the initial resistance to the Roman legions in the southeast. After his forces lost vital battles on the rivers Thames and Medway, he fled to Wales and continued to be a thorn in the Claudian flesh by assuming military leadership of the local Silures and Ordovices.

Where the tribes were

These were the major tribes in England when the Romans arrived:

Atrebates West Sussex, Hampshire, Berkshire

Brigantes Yorkshire, Cleveland, Durham, Lancashire

Cantiaci north and east Kent

Carvetii Cumbria

Catuvellauni Hertfordshire, Bedfordshire, south Cambridgeshire

Corieltauvi East Midlands

Cornovii Staffordshire, Shropshire, Cheshire

Dubunni Severn Valley and the Cotswolds as far south as the Mendips

Dumnonii The whole of the southwest peninsula and parts of Somerset

Durotriges Dorset and its surrounds

Iceni Norfolk and parts of Suffolk and Cambridgeshire

Parisi East Yorkshire

Trinovantes north of the Thames in Essex and Suffolk

The territories of the Regni (based at Chichester) and the Belgae (at Winchester) were artificially created by the Romans after the invasion of AD 43.

Defeated in battle in AD 51, Caratacus escaped to the Brigantes in Yorkshire, but Queen Cartimandua promptly handed him over to the Romans in chains – a great coup for them, because the capture of their most dangerous enemy effectively pacified southern England from the Humber to the Severn.

It was his spirit that saved Caratacus. Taken to Rome as a war prize, and expecting execution, he was allowed to plead for clemency before the Senate. The historian Tacitus records that he spoke proudly of his ancestry and asked some sharp questions: 'I had horses, men, arms and wealth – why wonder that I was unwilling to lose them? If you wish to subjugate everyone, does it follow that we should accept your slavery?'

Caratacus was pardoned and allowed to live in Rome. Dio Cassius, another historian, tells us that his admiration of the city prompted a further question: 'Can you, who have such possessions, and so many of them, covet our poor tents?' Ha! We've visited prosperous Iron Age Silchester, and if he really said that, he was simply playing to the gallery.

Within a few years the Romans had virtual control. In the forests and mountains of Wales the tribes were proving hard to dislodge (there were legions based at Chester and Wroxeter), and Scotland was a project for the future, but the south was largely subdued and the northern buffer zone was controlled by the Brigantes – fickle but currently loyal.

Remaindered Wroxeter

Most Roman towns (see page 53) kept growing, but Wroxeter – 5 miles (8 km) southeast of Shrewsbury in Shropshire – was one of the few which didn't.

Then called Viroconium, it began as a garrison to guard the Welsh border, and by the 2nd century AD had developed to become the fourth largest town in Britain. Its surrounding ramparts extended for 2 miles (8 km), its huge baths could accommodate a thousand visitors at a time, and it boasted a population of around 15,000 people.

It was abandoned some time after the Romans left, and today it's a small village with a redundant church – built, in part, with stone salvaged from that original town.

London's burning

The Iceni had once been loyal, too, but in AD 60 or 61 (accounts differ) the Romans brought trouble on their own heads by their treatment of Boudica (or Boadicea), the newly widowed wife of the tribe's leader, Prasutagus.

In his will Prasutagus had shared everything equally between his daughters and the emperor, but his wishes were completely ignored. The kingdom was annexed and Roman financiers called in their loans. Boudica was flogged and her daughters were raped. With the aid of the Trinovantes, she now led a revolt.

- **Camulodunum (Colchester) was destroyed and its Roman inhabitants killed.**
- **The IX Hispana Legion, sent to relieve the settlement, was routed.**
- **The Roman governor, Suetonius, abandoned Londinium, knowing that he was unable to defend it, and the town was burned to ashes.**
- **Next in line was Verulamium (St Albans) – and that was burned to the ground, too.**

The damage was so severe and the loss of life so great (an estimated 70,000 perished) that the emperor Nero considered withdrawing his forces from Britain, but Suetonius at last managed to defeat the rebel forces at the Battle of Watling Street. Boudica died – possibly by her own hand – and the crisis was averted.

Pensioned off

Camulodunum had been the capital of the Trinovantes tribe before the invasion, but the Romans built their first permanent legionary fortress there and then turned it into a *colonia*, or settlement for retired soldiers.

Tacitus tells us that the old soldiers were hated because they 'drove people out of their houses, ejected them from their farms and called them captives and slaves'.

It was no wonder, then, that when Boudica's rebels swarmed over the town they showed no mercy to these charmless usurpers.

Natural resources

The Romans must have calculated long and hard about the economic returns from their 'investment' in the invasion and the stationing of so many troops in hostile territory. How could they exploit the island's mineral wealth to recoup at least some of their outlay?

Athough Cornish tin had been exported in large quantities before the occupation, there was surprisingly little call for it now – the Roman conquest of northwest Spain had yielded ready supplies there instead. Copper and a little gold were mined in Wales, but elsewhere it was more humdrum stuff that turned a profit.

• **Lead**. You can tell that it was important because most of the mining was at first carried out directly by the Imperial government rather than being entrusted to tribal entrepreneurs. And *why* was it important? Because lead, through treatment under high temperatures (cupellation), was the only known way of producing silver – and silver was the foremost monetary exchange.

Date-stamped ingots reveal that the Mendip mines in Somerset were producing ore as early as AD 49. (It had a silver content of up to 0.4 per cent.) There were other large mines in Nidderdale, Yorkshire, and in Derbyshire, where some private lessees were allowed to get in on the act.

• **Iron**. This wasn't regarded as a valuable metal, and so its production wasn't restricted to Imperial agents, but it was a major industry nevertheless, flourishing chiefly in the Forest of Dean, the East Midlands and the Weald of Sussex and Kent.

Out-and-about tip: find the word 'bloomery' on an Ordnance Survey map to locate a site likely to contain traces of slag – a byproduct of the smelting process. The Romans used it for their roads.

The Classis Britannica, or British Fleet – a supply organisation as well as a navy – was directly involved in ironworking. Its operation at Beauport Park, on the edge of Hastings, is the third largest to have been found anywhere in the empire. The remains include a substantial bath-house, with some walls still standing to a height of 7 ft (2.1 m). The Romans were fond of inscriptions, and one here suggests that a man named Bassus was responsible for building it.

• **Coal**. Although coal was mined by the Romans, there's no evidence that it was regarded as worth exporting, and the only mention of it in their literature is to the fact that it was seen on the altars of Sulis Minerva at Aquae Sulis (see page 54). Wood and charcoal were the more common heating fuels.

• **Kimmeridge shale.** Mined from cliffs on the Isle of Purbeck in Dorset, this was valued for its use, when polished, in jewellery, dishes, decorative panels and even as (expensive) table legs with claw feet and seahorse shoulders.

• **Purbeck marble.** Its toughness made it an ideal base for grinding and pounding (many mortars have been found throughout Britain), but it was also widely used for those Roman monumental inscriptions, its speckled greyish-white making a good background for the vermilion lettering they favoured.

• **Whitby jet**. This distinctive material is found in lumps on the north Yorkshire coast. Magnetic when rubbed, it was believed to have healing qualities and to ward off the evil eye. York was a centre for the manufacture of carved pendants, bracelets, rings, hairpins – even the Roman equivalent of a teddy bear.

A Roman gazetteer

What we call their towns today

Aquae Sulis	Bath
Callera	Silchester
Camulodunum	Colchester
Corinium	Cirencester
Deva	Chester
Durnovaria	Dorchester
Durovernum	Canterbury
Eburacum	York
Glevum	Gloucester
Isca	Exeter
Isurium	Aldborough (N. Yorks.)
Lindum	Lincoln
Londinium	London
Noviomagus	Chichester
Ratae	Leicester
Venta	Winchester
Verulamium	St Albans
Viroconium	Wroxeter

Ancient curses

The waters of present-day Bath were renowned long before the Romans reached Somerset to lavish money and building skills on creating their own vision of a bathing paradise.

Local people had raised a shrine to the goddess Sulis at what is the only designated hot spring (46°C; 115°F) in all of Britain. The Romans identified her with their own goddess Minerva, but were happy to give her precedence in their naming of the place: Aquae Sulis.

Here they fashioned a complex of hot, warm and cold baths, sweat rooms with underfloor heating, changing rooms – and a temple.

Look out for objects thrown into the spring:

- Roman coins as offerings to the goddess. The total of more than 12,000 of them constitutes the largest votive deposit in Britain.
- Special metal urns known as *paterae*, probably used to make offerings of holy water.
- Curses inscribed on sheets of lead or pewter, which were rolled up and thrown into the spring. Many relate to the theft of clothing while the owner was bathing, and one of them is the only known example of a sentence written in the local Celtic tongue.

Taming the Barbarians

It's difficult to gauge how things changed for the average man, woman and child in England after the Romans came, but there's no doubt that many of them were introduced to urban living for the first time. We've seen that the inhabitants of Silchester (the better-off among them, at least) had long since been accustomed to a comfortable life, but existing towns expanded and new ones – such as Colchester, Chichester, Gloucester and Lincoln – were created from garrison beginnings.

They weren't, needless to say, anywhere near as grand as Rome or the other large cities of southern Europe. Lincoln was an exception, but the new citizens couldn't generally expect a fully fledged sewer system, and although a supply of clean water was regarded as essential – often via timber pipes held by iron collars – there were none of the majestic aqueducts which fed Roman towns in other parts of the empire, channelling water from springs many miles away. They all, though, had the regulation 'civilised' complement of forums, basilicas and public baths.

These urban and military centres were connected by the famously efficient system of Roman roads. For their long-distance journeys the Iron Age English had, for the most part, been content to use unpaved trackways on high, dry ground, but military engineers now created raised, metalled roads which marched across the countryside in confident, almost arrogant, straight lines.

The chief purpose of the major routes was to carry troops, supplies and the Imperial Post, while networks of smaller roads served the needs of local communities.

North and south

How much you felt oppressed by foreign rule depended on where you lived. As we've seen, there was an early aping of the Roman way of life in areas closest to the Continent. Here, if you were lucky, you would see soldiers only if they were passing through. If you lived in northern territory susceptible to tribal raids, on the other hand, you were potentially caught between the proverbial rock and a hard place.

from A to B

By AD 180 the Romans had completed their main network of major roads across Britain, stretching for about 2,000 miles (3,200 km). These were the principal English routes (they were given their present names much later):

- London to Dover via Canterbury
- London to Chichester (Stane Street)
- London to Silchester, with branches to:
  - Portchester via Winchester and Southampton
  - Exeter via Salisbury and Dorchester
  - Gloucester and Caerleon
- London to Chester via St Albans, Lichfield and Wroxeter
- London to York via Lincoln
- London to Bury St Edmunds via Colchester
- Lincoln to Exeter (Fosse Way)
- York to Gloucester (Icknield Street)
- Dover to Wroxeter (Watling Street)
- York to Chester, Wroxeter and Carlisle

The economies of the north and south were different, too. Togidubnus's Sussex acres, for instance, enjoyed great prosperity during the Roman heyday. The land was fertile, and farming estates with villas at their centre littered the downland landscape. While some of these villas never grew much beyond their humble beginnings, others – as at Bignor – became positively luxurious as their owners (all local men made good) expanded their rural empires.

Romano-British plonk

The English climate during the Roman occupation was warm enough to allow grape production. The wine they produced might not go down well at a modern dinner party, though.

- The grapes were picked before they were fully ripe, and then laced with honey for sweetness.
- The wine was probably fruity, sweet and brownish, about 10–12 per cent alcohol.
- It would have been drunk within six months after fermenting in barrels or amphorae (earthenware jars).

In the northern uplands, pastoralism – cattle, horses, sheep – had traditionally been much more important than agriculture. Whereas the Roman tax collector would count bushels of wheat in the south, he tallied animal heads and hides in the north. In the territory of the Brigantes and the neighbouring Parisi the development of Roman-style villas had to wait until early in the 4th century.

Here are five villas worth seeking out:

- **Bignor, West Sussex.** Close to Stane Street, it has finely wrought mosaics and, at 79 ft (24 m), the longest mosaic corridor in the country.
- **Brading, Isle of Wight.** Like Bignor, it dates from the 1st century AD, grew over time and has outstanding mosaics.
- **Chedworth, Gloucestershire.** One of the largest in Britain (and one of about fifty in the Cotswolds), it was built in stages from the 2nd to the 4th centuries.
- **Littlecote, Wiltshire.** A winged corridor villa most celebrated for its Orpheus mosaic, supposed to have pagan associations.
- **Lullingstone, Kent.** Begun around AD 80 and enlarged 70 years later, it may have been the country retreat of the provincial governor.

Life on the wall

The Romans were here for nearly 400 years, but in all that time they never managed to control the tribes of Caledonia, and the border between England and what we now know as Scotland was fluid and porous.

Twice, however, serious attempts were made to fix the line. The first, and most substantial, was Hadrian's Wall, completed in AD 128, between the Tyne and the Solway. The second (beyond the geographical bounds of our book) was the Antonine Wall, between the Forth and the Clyde: this was raised in AD 142, but after about 20 years the army was pulled back to Hadrian's formidable structure – the most heavily fortified border in the empire.

A few facts and figures:

- **The wall extended for 73 miles (120 km).**
- **It had small fortlets (roughly) every mile and 15 major forts, including two which have been extensively excavated: Housesteads and Vindolanda.**

- **East of the River Irthing it was made of stone and was 9 ft 9 in (3 m) wide and 16–20 ft (5–6 m) high.**

- **West of the Irthing it was turf, with walls 20 ft (6 m) wide and 11 ft 6 in (3.5 m) high.**

- **To the north there was a deep ditch and a row of pits with entanglements.**

- **South of the wall there was a military road and the *vallum* – a turf rampart with a deep outer ditch.**

Legionnaires built the wall, but it was manned by auxiliaries – non-Roman citizens recruited from tribes conquered in various parts of the empire. Outside each fort would be an encampment of women, children, merchants and slaves (a town in miniature), and the way they lived has been revealed by no fewer than 2,000 writing tablets retrieved by archaeologists from the anaerobic layer of soil beneath the Vindolanda fort – the earliest written archive in England. The Romans' slang name for the native barbarians appears in the written record at Vindolanda – *Brittunculi*, or 'wretched little Brits'.

Hundreds of individuals are named on these tablets, from the high (commanding officers) to the low (slaves, pig keepers, bath orderlies), while the subjects covered range from the weather – the northern frontier would be chilly for a southern European – to beer shortages, hunting expeditions, birthday parties and much more.

The soldiers' pay was international currency, and they could use it to buy goods and services either in settlements nearby or from their regimental quartermasters. They may have been far from home, and their letters contain occasional gripes about sickness, miscarriages of justice and poor roads holding up supplies, but the evidence suggests that they lived in much greater comfort than the native tribes in the villages beyond.

The wall continued to be manned throughout the Roman occupation of Britain, but by the late 4th century it must have seemed a little vainglorious as it swaggered across the landscape. It could still be used to regulate troublesome Picts, but by now there were troubles galore in other parts of England.

A lost legion

Rosemary Sutcliff's best-selling children's novel *The Eagle of the Ninth* is set in the 2nd century AD after the building of Hadrian's Wall. It tells the story of a young Roman officer on a quest to discover the truth about the disappearance of his father's legion in northern Britain.

Sutcliff drew on the supposed annihilation of the IX Hispana Legion in battle (though historians argue about where this happened, if it did at all) and on the discovery of a wingless Roman eagle in the excavations at Silchester.

Historians at the Museum of Reading, where the trophy is on display, tell us that it was probably part of a statue of Jupiter in the forum at Silchester rather than a legionary eagle – but few captivated readers will complain about the author's artistic licence.

How they worshipped in Roman times

When the Romans arrived, they found Celtic cults worshipping their own gods and goddesses, often under the leadership of priestly Druids. As we've seen at Aquae Sulis, they were happy to merge these native cults with their own, and votive shrines were a feature of the new Roman towns.

More controversial was the worship of the emperor, which the Romans introduced to Britain as a means of unifying the population in displays of loyalty. The historian Tacitus tells us that the implementation of this official religion was one cause of Boudica's sacking of Colchester.

The early Christians refused to bow the knee to the emperor, and for centuries they were persecuted, but in AD 313 Emperor Constantine the Great legalised Christianity, and in 380 it became the offical religion of the empire.

Christian relics in England from the Roman period include wall paintings at the Lullingstone villa in Kent, a mosaic from a villa at Frampton in Dorset, and objects bearing the *Chi-Rho (XP)* symbol in the hoards discovered at Water Newton in Cambridgeshire and Mildenhall in Suffolk.

Endgame

Challenges to the authority of Rome came from both inside the province and without. In its heyday the empire was ruled by strong men who managed to keep it more or less unified, despite its vast size. As strains on the system grew ever more severe, anyone with an army saw a chance of ruling the world:

- In AD 193 the emperor Commodus was assassinated, and the governor of Britain, Clodius Albinus, took his army to the Continent in a (failed) attempt to land the prize. While he was away the northern tribes swarmed over Hadrian's Wall and sacked English towns as far south as York.

- In AD 287 Carausius, commander of the British Fleet, usurped power, declaring himself emperor of Britain and northern Gaul. He was assassinated by his finance minister, Allectus, seven years later.

- In AD 383 the Spaniard Magnus Maximus went one better, being proclaimed emperor in Britain by the Roman troops; leading his army into Italy itself; and being recognised as 'Augustus in the West', with control over Britain, Gaul, Spain and Africa.

All the time that these ruthless men were treating Britain as a useful base from which to launch their personal ambitions, the people they were supposed to protect were being besieged not only by the Caledonian tribes in the north, but increasingly by land- and loot-hungry Saxon pirates along the coasts of the south and east.

From AD 287 Carausius, both admiral and self-styled emperor, instigated a series of coastal defences known as the Saxon Shore – forts and ramparts running from Norfolk round to the Isle of Wight. Both soldiers and sailors manned these establishments. Nippy scout-ships, painted sea-green, were manned by crews of 20 rowers dressed in the same colour, their job being to report the movements of any marauders.

Things grew steadily worse. In AD 367 the Saxons, Picts and Scots joined forces to break through Hadrian's Wall and kill the coastal defence chief, the Count of the Saxon Shore. There were suggestions of treachery by frontier scouts, tempted by the spoils, and many soldiers deserted.

Now new forts were built on the Yorkshire coast, with tall lookout towers, and northern tribes were given increased independence as treaty states in order to encourage a necessary spirit of self-defence.

It was no use. These measures might have kept the raiders at bay for a while, but the empire itself was crumbling, and in AD 410 Rome announced the withdrawal of its troops. The Brittunculi were on their own.

King Arthur: the Saxons' greatest leader, or just the stuff of legend?

Chapter Three

SAXON ROOTS

They poured into a country newly abandoned by the Roman legions, rowing up the rivers to annex fertile farmland and putting to the sword anyone foolhardy enough to get in their way. Migrating from homelands gradually being eaten up by the sea, the Angles, Saxons, Frisians and Jutes forced the Romano-British natives to retreat westwards to the 'Celtic fringe' of Wales and Cornwall until scarcely a trace of them remained.

Or so the traditional story used to run…

Knights of the Round Table

If there ever was a King Arthur, he was a Celtic war leader defending his territory against the Saxons in the years after the Romans left Britain. Geoffrey of Monmouth's fanciful 12th-century *Historia Regum Britanniae* relayed the most influential early version of the legendary chieftain and his Round Table, and the romance has been a staple of books, poems, paintings and films ever since.

Gildas (see facing page) makes no mention of Arthur – his hero is named Ambrosius Aurelianus – but medieval writers couldn't resist making him the hero of the Battle of Mount Badon, which some writers have suggested was fought not far from Bath.

And where was Camelot? There's been no shortage of claimants to that throne:

- Cadbury Castle hill fort, near the village of Queen Camel, Somerset
- Caerwent
- Camaret, Brittany
- Camboglanna fort on Hadrian's Wall
- Camelford, Cornwall
- Campus Elleti, Glamorgan
- Tintagel Castle, Cornwall
- Winchester.

Like many a gripping but doubtful tale, this one contains elements of the truth while madly oversimplifying. These people *did* arrive, but it seems that some of them were already here during the Roman period, employed as mercenaries to defend the coast, and that others arrived with the same remit once the legions had gone. According to this version, it was only when their hosts failed to pay them that they turned nasty and began to seize swaths of land for themselves.

Our evidence for 'what happened next' is decidedly patchy. Here are three sources:

The British monk Gildas (c. 500–570), the closest to the events, tells us that the Celts put up stiff resistance to the invaders, and stemmed the tide for a while by winning the Battle of Mount Badon around 500 – but he doesn't tell us where this was.

In his *Historia Ecclesiastica Gentis Anglorum* (Ecclesiastical History of the English People), the Venerable Bede (c. 672–735) confidently places the incomers in various areas of England – the Angles in today's East Anglia and up the east coast to Northumberland; the Jutes in Kent; the Saxons in Essex, Sussex and points west – but he was writing well over 300 years later. Although archaeologists have noted small differences in burial customs in those early settlement years, the various groups merged culturally within a fairly short period – so, employing a reasonable shorthand, we shall refer to them all as Anglo-Saxons.

The *Anglo-Saxon Chronicle*, detailed though it is about the centuries after the Romans left, dates from the late 9th century. It follows Bede in claiming that a tribal leader named Vortigern employed the Germanic warriors Hengist and Horsa to protect his territory, and that they later turned against him.

We've already noted the genetic evidence for the continuity of native bloodlines, and the best guess today is that the newcomers mingled and interbred with the British Celts. Battles there undoubtedly were, and the Anglo-Saxons ruled the roost, but the two peoples learned to rub along together. And those western Celtic strongholds? The invaders simply hadn't got there yet.

The most remarkable late survival of a Celtic culture was the kingdom of Elmet in what later became the West Riding of Yorkshire. Here the natives held out against the Anglo-Saxon advance until the early 7th century, when they succumbed to the Northumbrians. The people of Elmet spoke the Brythonic form of the Celtic language common to Wales and Cornwall, and the name of their enclave survives near Leeds in the parishes of Sherburn-in-Elmet, Barwick-in-Elmet and Scholes-in-Elmet.

Arthur's *last* stand?

Wansdyke in the west of England is an impressive east–west defensive earthwork, the section from Savernake Forest to Morgan's Hill in Wiltshire dating from the years of the Anglo-Saxon invasion. The bank still stands 13 ft (4 m) high, above a ditch 8 ft (2.5 m) deep, and runs for all of 9 miles (14 km).

The dyke picks up again further west, and this section is thought to be the Celtic–Saxon border established after the Battle of Deorham, near Gloucester, in 577.

Country folk

The Anglo-Saxons were a rural people, and they had little time for the Roman urban heritage. They would no doubt have used the long, straight roads when travelling between the existing towns, but their new settlements were in the countryside, where they built in timber rather than stone.

Even when they did set up home within the secure walls of a city such as London, they put up wooden houses among the gradually decaying Roman buildings – partly, no doubt, because they lacked the expertise to repair them.

This lack of know-how perhaps accounts for the abandonment of many a Roman villa in the years that followed. A typical Saxon 'village' in these early days was very small – just a handful of families – and the evidence suggests that most farmers were happier starting afresh rather than inhabiting a building whose fancy mosaics, underfloor heating and plumbing they were unable to maintain. And how could a new owner have bought replacements, even if he had known how to install them? We have to imagine small bands of settlers rather than a centrally organised workforce, and to realise that for hundreds of years after their arrival most Saxons had no common currency with which to trade. These pioneers needed to be self-sufficient, filling their stomachs by tilling their own fields and managing their own flocks and herds.

The work of giants

A lament for the glory that was Rome appears in the 8th-century Old English poem *The Ruin*. The writer's mention of hot-water baths almost certainly refers to Aquae Sulis, and his awe – 'the work of giants crumbles' – suggests that he knew nothing of the people who had created such a wonder 'a hundred generations' earlier.

He has a brave stab at imagining them, evoking streets lined with bath-houses and riotous mead-halls, until cruel Fate intervenes:

> Days of pestilence came.
> Death took all the brave men away.
> The places of war were deserted
> And the city decayed.

The heptarchy malarky

You'll be relieved to learn that we're not going to dig deep into the endlessly exhausting political infighting during the centuries of Anglo-Saxon rule in England. For the sake of convenience historians used to refer to the so-called 'heptarchy', a territorial split between seven kingdoms – the three giants of Northumbria, Mercia and Wessex, plus Kent, East Anglia, Essex and Sussex.

The Dark Ages

That's what these early Anglo-Saxon years used to be called. For some, this was because so little was known about them, and it's true that historians and archaeologists still have to work hard to piece together relatively scanty pieces of evidence from the period.

The predominant implication, however, was that the pagan Saxons existed in a regrettable black spot between the enlightenment of the Roman Empire and the glories of the Christianised Renaissance. This kind of value judgement is now frowned upon – which means that you won't often hear the term used today.

Today it's recognised that there were subtle shiftings between various mini-kingdoms over time, but here's a nutshell guide to Anglo-Saxon arm-wrestling. (There won't be a test paper at the end of it.)

Kent was the leading power in the land at the end of the 6th century, but soon gave way to **East Anglia**, whose King Raedwald (see pages 78–79) attempted to extend his power north of the Humber.

He failed. **Northumbria** – covering a large part of the northeast – was cock of the roost under Edwin and Oswald, and came close to controlling the whole of England.

Hands-on history: Visit the hamlet of Yeavering, Northumberland (Bede's 'Gefrin'), where archaeologists have found one of Edwin's palaces.

Mercia, under King Wulfhere, put a stop to that. His kingdom straddled the Midlands, but before the end of the 7th century it had swallowed Essex and East Anglia and also controlled London, by now a great mercantile centre.

Sutton Hoo

The early 7th-century ship burial excavated at Sutton Hoo in Suffolk is so magnificent in its trappings that many historians confidently proclaim it to be the last resting place of Raedwald, the great Anglo-Saxon king who ruled East Anglia from 599 until his death around 624.

Set among the mounds of two 6th- and 7th-century cemeteries on the banks of the River Deben near Woodbridge, it lay completely undisturbed until modern times. The oak timbers had rotted, but nearly all the iron planking rivets remained in place, and stains in the sand preserved the details of its construction.

- It was 89 ft (27 m) long, pointed at each end, and 14 ft (4.4 m) wide amidships.
- Repairs were visible, showing that it had been a genuine seagoing vessel.
- It had been hauled uphill from the river and lowered into a trench so that only the tops of the stem and stern posts rose above the surface, before it was covered by an oval mound.

The form of the ship burial and the military equipment within it have close affinities with southern Swedish practices of the same period.

Although the absence of a body at first led to theories that this was a cenotaph, soil analyses have since found traces of phosphate, supporting the theory that human remains had sunk into the acidic soil. There were also signs of a platform or large coffin some 9 ft (2.7 m) long, with a lamp, bucket and bottle close by.

The grave goods deposited in the burial chamber are of a dazzlingly high quality:

- the famous helmet with an iron skull, a full face mask, deep cheek pieces and panels of tinned bronze

- a nested set of ten silver bowls, probably made in the Eastern Empire in the 6th century, together with two silver spoons

- a sword inside a decorated scabbard, its harness and belt richly ornamented with gold mounts and strap-distributors displaying intricate garnet cellwork

- a large silver platter with chased ornament, made in the Eastern Empire around 500 and bearing the official stamps of the emperor Anastasius.

These and many more treasures now rest in the British Museum in London, but copies are on display at a permanent exhibition close to where they were found.

The great Mercian leader Offa (757–796) constructed a massive dyke running along the Welsh border – up to 8 ft (2.4 m) high and 65 ft (19.8 m) wide – either as a defensive wall or as an emphatic boundary marker.

It was the turn of **Wessex** early in the 9th century, with Egbert defeating the Mercians in 825 at the Battle of Ellendun, a site unknown but probably south of Swindon in Wiltshire. The historian Sir Frank Stenton described it as 'one of the most decisive battles of English history', cementing the power of a kingdom soon to play a vital role in defending the fledgling Saxon nation against a vicious, implacable enemy.

A man with a mission

First, though, we take a step back in time to another vital date in English history – to 597, when St Augustine landed on the Isle of Thanet on his mission to convert the people of Kent to Christianity.

Many native Celts already had their own form of the religion, of course, first introduced to them during the latter years of the Roman occupation. Augustine, arriving with the authority of Pope Gregory the Great, simply gave them the cold shoulder. His business was with the people who counted – the Anglo-Saxon rulers of the island – and he began with a soft target. King Aethelbert of Kent had married a Christian princess and was therefore receptive to his approaches.

Augustine triumphed. That Christmas Day, already installed as the first archbishop of Canterbury, he baptised literally thousands of converts in a mass ceremony. The king of Essex soon followed Kent's lead, and Raedwald of East Anglia initially signed up, too – although he met opposition from his pagan wife and compromised by maintaining, as the Venerable Bede put it, 'one altar for Christian worship and another for sacrifice to devils'.

Pope Gregory now stepped up his campaign by sending more missionaries to England, establishing bishops at London and Rochester and founding a training school for Anglo-Saxon priests and missionaries.

The flight of a sparrow

The Venerable Bede's account of Edwin's conversion includes a speech made by an unnamed nobleman, arguing – with vivid imagery – that the new doctrine offered some certainty in a hostile world:

> Our life seems to me like the swift flight of a sparrow through a winter banqueting room where you sit around a blazing fire among your thegns [retainers] and counsellors while storms of rain and snow rage outside. This sparrow flies in at one door and immediately out of another. While inside, it is safe from the wintry elements, but it immediately vanishes out of sight into the dark winter from which it came. So appears this brief life of man – of what went before or what is to follow we are quite ignorant.

William Wordsworth has a version of the story in his *Ecclesiastical Ballads*:

> Man's life is like a Sparrow, mighty King!
> That – while at banquet with your Chiefs you sit,
> Housed near a blazing fire – is seen to flit
> Safe from the wintry tempest. Fluttering,
> Here did it enter; there, on hasty wing,
> Flies out, and passes on from cold to cold;
> But whence it came we know not, nor behold
> Whither it goes.

One by one the Anglo-Saxon kings bent the knee to Rome, albeit not without controversy. Edwin of Northumbria was converted by Paulinus, who became Bishop of York, but the king's successors renounced the deal. (It was later reinstated by Oswald.) The Mercian leader Penda, who killed both Edwin and Oswald in battle, kept his kingdom resolutely pagan, but his sons adopted Christianity after his death in 655.

The last of the heptarchs to fall into line was Sussex, converted by St Wilfrid in 681. While not geographically distant from Augustine's see at Canterbury, it was separated from Kent by the dense forest of Andredsweald.

Wilfrid, Bishop of York, was the original blunt northerner, his career punctuated by spats with the English kings. He came to the south coast while exiled from Northumbria, set up a diocese for the South Saxons at Selsey and began organising the spread of the newly adopted religion throughout a countryside which barely knew it. Bede tells us that he also taught the local people to fish – but we should surely take that with a pinch of sea salt.

Christian hair-splitting

The peppery Wilfrid of course threw himself into the acrimonious debate that now developed between the two forms of Christianity operating in England – the native Celtic 'insular' variety and the Roman one. Pope Gregory had hoped that Augustine would be his metropolitan archbishop with authority over all southern England, but the British bishops resisted such a takeover.

At a series of meetings Augustine made three demands of them:

1. They should adopt the Roman method of fixing the date of Easter. (In King Oswiu's Northumberland, evangelised by both Irish and Roman missionaries, some Christians found themselves fasting for Lent while their co-religionists celebrated the Resurrection.)

2. They should reform their baptismal rite. (Bede says it was 'incomplete', without further explanation.)

3. They should play an active role in the mission to the Anglo-Saxons, rather than stay at home in the comfort of their monasteries.

There was a further niggling argument about hairstyles, which – although not a doctrinal issue – brought the two sides aggressively head-to-head. Monks in the Roman tradition cut their locks into the tonsure with which we're familiar today: a bald crown at the centre. Quite how the British did it isn't clear, but they shaved their heads from ear to ear in some fashion – and they liked it that way!

The Lindisfarne Gospels

A glory of the early Anglo-Saxon Christian period is an illuminated manuscript produced on the 'Holy Island' of Lindisfarne.

The Lindisfarne Gospels are thought to have been created by Eadfrith, a monk who became bishop of Lindisfarne in 698 – perhaps in honour of his predecessor St Cuthbert, the patron saint of northern England, who died a hermit on nearby Farne Island in 687.

The Gospels are richly illustrated in the 'insular' style (that is, they take their inspiration from British rather than European art). Billfrith, an anchorite, fashioned a leather binding for it, studded with jewels and metals, but this was lost during Viking raids.

Wilfrid famously, and victoriously, took the Roman line at the 664 Synod of Whitby, called by King Oswiu of Northumbria to decide which of the two traditions the kingdom should follow. His defeated opponent was Colmán, then Bishop of Lindisfarne, who afterwards packed his bags, gathered up some relics of St Aidan and retired to Ireland, where he founded a monastery.

The first poet?

The humble lay brother Caedmon, who looked after the animals at Whitby Abbey in the late 7th century, is generally acclaimed as the first Anglo-Saxon poet – although our only written evidence is a nine-line hymn in Bede's *History*.

Bede tells us that the gift came to him in a dream, after which the untutored Caedmon created alliterative verse 'of much sweetness and humility in English, which was his native language'.

The upshot was a heady promotion. He took monastic vows, and the abbess had him taught sacred history and doctrine so that he could give them poetic expression.

The making of England

Weaning the Anglo-Saxons from their pagan gods was a gradual and patchy affair, but the spread of a literate, legalistic and bureaucratic clergy into all parts of the country played a profound role in the creation of a recognisably homogeneous culture – in the creation, that is, of England.

Yes, there were still bloody power struggles between rival kingdoms, but increasingly an inhabitant of one could cross into the other without the uneasiness of feeling 'foreign'. Not only did these proto-English men and women share a religion, but they spoke a common tongue and, from the late 7th century, used a common currency: the silver *sceatta*.

They shared a broadly similar law system, too. Kings called meetings of the **Witan**, to discuss national events with their nobles and advisors; village representatives attended **moots** to thrash out local affairs; and alleged offenders were called to account before the **hundred** – a court named after an administrative area with sufficient land to support a hundred families.

How the Anglo-Saxons dealt with crime

Justice took many forms in Anglo-Saxon England, with jail not a common option:

- Each party in a dispute could muster oath-helpers to swear his own innocence or his opponent's guilt, and in a small community where both were known this was often sufficient to secure a verdict.

- If he protested his innocence despite the oath-taking going against him, he could opt for trial by ordeal. In the cold water ordeal he would be thrown into deep water and would be considered innocent if he sank to the bottom. The hot water and iron ordeals involved having a hand burned, innocence being proved if the wound healed promptly.

- *Weregild* was paid to compensate the victims of robbery, injury and accidental death. The price rose according to the importance of the person killed, with slaves effectively counting for nothing.

- Murder, arson and treachery to one's lord were among the 'bootless' (irremediable) crimes which attracted the death penalty.

- Other punishments included mutilation – mainly the chopping off of hands and noses.

It's impossible to gauge how tough life was for the great majority whose social status lay between noble and slave. Many lived in 'nucleated' villages, their houses clustering around a church and a green. Families shared common fields to grow barley, oats and wheat which were locally milled for the table, flax for cloth-making and woad for dyeing. They tended sheep, cattle, pigs and goats, and lived in thatched wooden huts with sunken floors.

What strikes us today is the continuity between the landscape these sturdy colonisers inhabited and our own. They had themselves at times followed existing Celtic boundaries, shared Romano-British cemeteries and built their churches on the sites of pagan altars, but we have only glimpses of this adaptability. Thanks to the considerable volume of legal charters from the period, on the other hand, we can plot their communal bounds, fields and meeting places, often with minute precision – and often the names have barely changed.

The same applies to our English towns and villages in those areas continuously controlled by the Anglo-Saxons before the Norman

Conquest. Not only were nearly all of them already in existence then, but their names are packed with clues about their origins. Here's a list of twenty telltale prefixes and suffixes, with their meanings:

bourn/burn	stream (*Bournemouth*)
burgh/bury	fortified place (*Banbury*)
combe	small valley (*Ilfracombe*)
cot/cote	shelter/cottage (*Swadlincote*)
dean/den	swine pasture (*Tenterden*)
dun	hill (*Dunster*)
ey/ney	island (*Pevensey*)
folk	people (*Suffolk*)
ham	village (*Streatham*)
hurst	wooded hill (*Hurstpierpoint*)
ing	people (of) (*Hastings*)
ley/lea	woodland clearing (*Crawley*)
mere	lake, pool (*Windermere*)
stan	stone (*Stanmore*)
stead	place/site (*Stansted*)
stoke	outlying farm (*Basingstoke*)
stow	meeting place (*Stowmarket*)
ton/tun	enclosure, village (*Preston*)
wick	farm (*Alnwick*)
worth	fenced land (*Tamworth*)

Towards the close of the 8th century this fast-maturing English society must have felt comfortable in its collective skin: civilised, prosperous and even (for the many who accepted the Christian faith) blessed by God.

And then, on what started out as just another ordinary day in the year 787, an official rode down from Dorchester in Dorset to welcome three Norwegian ships which had moored at Portland Bay. Expecting to talk business with traders, he was unceremoniously killed on the spot.

The poor man had encountered a new breed of visitors, and he was but the first among thousands who would perish at their hands. The Vikings had arrived.

We will fight them on the beaches ~ the Vikings shatter the peace of Anglo-Saxon England

CHAPTER FOUR

NEW KIDS ON THE BLOCK

It was in 793 that their longships first appeared on the horizon off Lindisfarne, bristling with warriors intent on ruthless plunder – and revenge.

The sheer terror experienced by monks going about their daily business at St Cuthbert's monastery is captured by the Northumbrian scholar Alcuin, then serving at the court of the emperor Charlemagne: 'The heathens poured out the blood of the saints around the altar and trampled on the bodies of saints in the temple of God, like dung in the streets.'

For the scribes who began to compile the *Anglo-Saxon Chronicle* a century later, that first Viking assault was still seared in the collective memory. There had already been omens in the guise of violent whirlwinds and storms of sheet lightning, 'and fiery dragons were seen flying in the sky'.

Dragon Ships

The Viking longships – used for trade as well as troop-carrying – were sleek, fast and so shallow in the draft that with 60 men on board they could navigate waterways only 3 ft (1 m) deep. The Anglo-Saxons knew them as 'dragon ships' because of their magnificently carved bows.

- They were fitted with oars the length of the boat, but later versions also had a rectangular sail on a single mast and could travel 50 miles (80 km) in a day.
- Double-ended, with a symmetrical bow and stern, they could reverse direction swiftly without having to turn around.
- They travelled at up to 15 knots (28 kph).
- They were so light that they could be carried inland.

These vicious Danes looted Lindisfarne of its treasures and were back along the northeast coast the following year to burn the monastery of St Paul at Jarrow – although on that occasion their leader was caught and put to death by the not-so-gentle monks. The monks also killed the luckless members of his raiding party who had been shipwrecked in a violent storm while trying to escape.

And that element of revenge? Not only had the Frankish emperor Charlemagne led a campaign against northern pagans, destroying their sanctuaries and shrines and cutting down their holy tree, but it was from this very island of Lindisfarne that Christian missionaries had set out to convert the pagan Norse people.

'Deliver us, Lord, from the savage Northmen who lay waste our land,' ran an antiphonal prayer of the beleaguered Anglo-Saxons.

This chapter covers a period of nearly 300 years during which the English fought, accommodated and eventually succumbed to these raiders and settlers from Denmark and Norway – without losing their own identity.

Brutality

The next few paragraphs are not for the squeamish. The English monks who recorded the repeated Viking assaults may well have exaggerated some of the horrors, but there's no doubting their basic savagery. These were trained fighters wielding battleaxes and fearsome double-edged swords, advancing behind kite-shaped shields. Some were known as 'berserkers' for the sheer abandon of their frenzied attacks.

- **A particularly ghastly torture was the 'blood eagle', its victim having his back cut open, his ribs cut and pulled apart and his lungs dragged out and draped over his shoulders. Oh, and salt was then sprinkled in the wounds.**
- **Women and children weren't spared, and one warrior became known as 'the children's man' because for some strange reason he refused to impale babies on his spear.**

These nasties come from Icelandic sagas, so it's impossible to say how commonly they were practised. The Anglo-Saxons, however, could be just as blood-curdling:

- When the red-bearded and splendidly named Ragnar Lodbrok ('Hairy-Breeks') was shipwrecked off Northumbria, he was thrown into a dungeon slithering with vipers. (His kinsmen exacted swift revenge.)

- In response to an attack by Svein 'Forkbeard' in 1002, all the Danes who had by now settled peaceably in eastern England were put to the sword in the St Brice's Day massacre. Svein's sister was among the dead, despite a desperate appeal to the king.

A talking wolf

King Edmund of East Anglia became the martyr St Edmund after his death at the hands of the Vikings in 869. It's possible that he was simply killed in battle, but legend says that he bravely refused to recant his Christianity and was therefore cruelly tortured – first beaten, then riddled with arrows and finally beheaded.

One version tells us that his head was thrown into a forest, but that his followers found it after hearing a wolf cry 'Here, here, here!'

A cult grew up around his relics, which during the 11th century were transferred to a shrine in the church at Bury St Edmunds.

Here to stay

For several decades these rapacious butchers had been content to harrass the coastal regions of England at unpredictable intervals, but in 865 they landed with a different kind of menace – possibly in response to the grim death-by-snakebite treatment delivered to Ragnar Lodbrok.

This time the 'great host' or 'heathen army' had wives and children following behind. There were thousands of them in hundreds of ships. Smash-and-grab booty was no longer enough: they had decided to settle.

The fighting men quickly subdued East Anglia. London they had already burned to the ground some years earlier, and now they swung north to seize a town known as Eburacum to the Romans, Eoforwic to the Saxons and York to us: to them it was Jorvik, or 'port of the chieftains' – it would remain their capital for close on a hundred years. With Northumbria tamed, they seized Reading and prepared to overwhelm the only Saxon kingdom still left on its feet: Wessex.

How they fought in Viking times

The terrifying nature of pitched battles in the Viking age is vividly expressed in the surviving fragment of an Old English poem, *The Battle of Maldon* – an account of a real battle fought on 11 August 991 on the banks of the River Blackwater in Essex.

- The Anglo-Saxon forces are drawn up in a line of battle behind a shield wall.
- The fighting begins with a hail of arrows and javelins, and then involves brutal hand-to-hand encounters with swords and spears.
- When shields are broken, the warriors continue to advance, loyalty to their lord making retreat unthinkable.

The battle-hardened Byrhtnoth, commanding the Anglo-Saxon forces, utters a brave speech as defeat becomes inevitable: 'Purpose shall be firmer, hearts more valiant, courage greater as strength grows weaker.'

It was, in short, a bloodbath, and Byrhtnoth was killed. He had been a patron of Ely Cathedral, and the grateful monks took his body for burial there.

Alfred the Great

The man charged with delivering the English people and their culture from seemingly inevitable subjection to the Viking yoke wasn't the warrior type at all. The picture which arises from the contemporary biography by Bishop Asser is of a bookish figure with lifelong health problems – possibly Crohn's disease.

Alfred (849–899) became king of Wessex in 871 only because all three of his older brothers had died – and if ever there was a poisoned chalice, this was it. In his very first year at the helm he had to fight no fewer than nine battles, and he lost most of them.

He reached his lowest ebb in January 878, when he was one of the few survivors of a lightning Viking attack on his royal stronghold at Chippenham, Wiltshire. He retreated to the marshes of Athelney in Somerset – where, according to legend, he came upon a peasant woman in her hovel, agreed to watch over her cakes and, preoccupied with his troubles, allowed them to burn.

It's impossible not to be stirred by the image of Alfred and his small band of survivors plotting the deliverance of their nation in the small fort they built on the Somerset Levels. It has the smack of Arthurian romance, even to its West Country location, with Alfred as the once and future king.

What followed was not only improbable but magnificent – a stunning victory followed by a reign renowned for its military, administrative and literary brilliance.

The victory came at Ethandun (present-day Edington, Wiltshire) in May 878, only months after that tail-between-legs retreat. Alfred had mustered a large force from Somerset, Wiltshire and Hampshire, and they totally overpowered a smaller Danish army, its survivors retreating inside the walls of Chippenham.

Alfred now employed a patient scorched-earth policy, destroying any food supplies the Vikings might gather in sudden forays from their fortress. Having starved them into submission, he forced the Viking leader Guthrum to sign a remarkable agreeement.

In the immediate aftermath of his surrender, Guthrum pledged to convert to Christianity. Three weeks later he and 29 of his men were baptised at Alfred's court near Athelney, and the Viking leader was adopted as the king's godson.

More significantly for English history, the two men later signed a treaty – to this day preserved in Old English at Corpus Christi College, Cambridge – which divided the country between them.

The Alfred Jewel

In 1693 a beautiful Anglo-Saxon ornament – part of it filigree gold – was discovered at North Petherton, Somerset, some 8 miles (13 km) from Athelney. It dates from King Alfred's era and is inscribed with the words 'Aelfred mec heht gewyrcan', or 'Alfred had me made'.

One theory is that it's from one of the precious staffs Alfred sent to each bishopric with a copy of his translation of Pope Gregory the Great's *Pastoral Care*. The jewel can now be seen in the Ashmolean Museum, Oxford.

'All of us estimate Englishman and Dane at the same amount,' reads a line in the treaty.

Various bands of Viking raiders would ignore the deal over the years, so that a battle was never far away, but the line held for generations. Guthrum and his successors were to occupy the area known as the Danelaw: East Anglia, the eastern part of Mercia, and most of the north and northeast. Wessex had the rest, except for Cornwall, which was still held by the Britons.

The boundary chiefly followed natural features and Roman roads: up the Thames to the River Lea; along the Lea to its source near Luton; in a straight line to Bedford; and then along the Ouse to Watling Street (see page 57).

London was given to Alfred, and he soon set about restoring the city to a habitable state, probably with a new street plan and certainly with new fortifications to complement the surviving Roman walls. Its name was changed from Lundenwic (denoting a trading place) to Lundenburh, reflecting its role as a vital link in a new chain of defensive towns.

Alfred, who ruled from Winchester, was determined that his territory should never again be vulnerable to surprise attack. A civilised, well-read man, he was also deeply conscious of what damage the Viking raids had inflicted on both the actual and cultural fabric of his kingdom. His adroit tackling of these problems during the last twenty years of his life earned him – uniquely among English monarchs – the soubriquet 'Great'.

- **He built a chain of some thirty fortified *burhs* around the borders of Wessex, most of which later developed into fully fledged towns such as Lewes, Wallingford and Wareham.**

- **To achieve this, Alfred expropriated some church lands and taxed landowners, who had to provide, feed and equip large numbers of men to build and maintain the walls.**

- **Rather than raise last-minute militias, or *fyrds*, from the shires, he created a standing army. A study of a contemporary document, the Burghal Hidage, suggests that one in four free men were enlisted at any one time.**

- **With attack likely to come from the sea, he created an effective navy, designing longships twice the length of their Viking counterparts.**

- He established a new code of law, though drawing on the best of the past – 'those that pleased me; and many of the ones that did not please me, I rejected with the advice of my councillors, and commanded them to be observed in a different way.'

- Lamenting the fact that learning had declined to the extent that hardly a single clerk could read Latin, Alfred invited scholars from the Continent, set up schools and had translated into Anglo-Saxon those Latin texts 'most necessary for all men to know'. Indeed, he translated some of them himself, and commissioned the *Anglo-Saxon Chronicle* so his people should know their own story.

Where the Witan met

Excavations at Cheddar, Somerset, from 1960 uncovered the remains of a royal palace mentioned in King Alfred's will.

The Witan (or national council) met here in 941, 956 and 968, and the discovery of an impressive 12th-century hall demonstrated that it remained an important site for several centuries. Royal ownership continued until 1209, when King John gave the manor to the Bishop of Bath and Wells.

Beowulf

We don't know who wrote the powerful Old English poem *Beowulf*, or even when it was written (almost certainly at some time between the 8th and early 11th centuries), but there's common agreement that the monster-slaying story is set in 6th-century Scandinavia – quite possibly the home of its author's ancestors.

The bloody tale can be simply told. Beowulf, a hero of the North Germanic Geats, comes to the aid of the Danish king Hrothgar whose mead hall is being attacked by a troll-like horror named Grendel. Beowulf defeats Grendel in unarmed combat, wrenching his arm off, but then has to contend with his fearsome mother – a lake-dwelling creature whom Beowulf eventually decapitates in her underwater lair. Many years later, Beowulf, now king of the Geats, has to deal with another monster. This time it's a dragon. He kills it, but is mortally wounded himself.

Beowulf and Grendel

Stressed out

There's a rugged vitality to Old English verse. It doesn't use rhyme, but depends for its emphasis on four heavy stresses in each line, two each either side of a short pause, or caesura. Usually at least three of the stressed words alliterate – that is, start with the same sound – making it ideal for vigorous declaiming.

It also uses metaphors consisting of formulaic compound phrases called *kennings*. *Beowulf* contains more than a thousand of them, including:

bone-house (body)
raven-harvest (corpse)
ring-giver (king)
slaughter-dew (blood)
wave-floater (ship)
whale-way (the sea)

Here's a brief snatch of the poem, with Beowulf being savaged by the dragon. Ouch!

Then the persecutor of people   pounced for a third time,
The fearsome fire-dragon   stirred again for the fight.
Seizing its chance   to challenge the champion,
Savage and spiteful   it spiked his neck
With awful fangs.   Out flowed the life-blood,
Bedewing his body: it came bubbling up.

The Danelaw

The learning which Alfred encouraged in his now secure kingdom of Wessex seems not to have been a priority in those areas held by Vikings, which means that the story of the Danelaw chiefly draws on Anglo-Saxon sources rather than the words of people who lived there.

Even their coins betray the illiteracy of the Viking world, with moneyers often unable to make sense of inscriptions they were copying, and so producing garbled gibberish.

This isn't to suggest that the Danelaw was inefficiently organised. It had its own legal codes, which applied from East Anglia up to Northumbria and throughout the 'Five Boroughs' of Leicester, Lincoln, Nottingham, Derby and Stamford, annexed from Mercia.

Although most Scandinavian inhabitants of the Danelaw were Danish, as the name implies, many of those in the northwest were Norwegians who had emigrated from their colony in Ireland.

It seems that the common man may have got a better deal in the Danelaw than elsewhere. Peasants had individual landownings called *sokes*, which owed services and taxes to the local lord but weren't under his direct control.

Reading the runes

Runes – thick vertical or angular symbols – were used to write Germanic languages before the Latin alphabet was adopted, and they persisted into the medieval period.

The Anglo-Saxon version – known as *futhork*, after the first few letters of the alphabet – appears on an ornamental 9th-century knife-blade found in the Thames. On one side is the only known complete inscription of the 28-letter alphabet, plus the owner's name: Beagnoth.

Northumbria had a 33-letter alphabet. The symbols not only represented sounds, but had their own individual, even magical, meanings.

Runes appear on 6th-century coins minted in Mercia and East Anglia, while the inscription on a comb-case found in Lincoln reads 'Thorfast made a good comb.'

There was an interesting difference in the fines for killing a man (*weregild*) in the two parts of England. Under Anglo-Saxon law this was assessed according to the rank of the victim's lord; in the Danelaw the man's own rank was the deciding factor.

The biggest dump

Archaeological excavations in the Coppergate area of York have given us invaluable insights into the prolonged Viking settlement there. Many finds are on display at the Jorvik Viking Centre, run by the York Archaeological Trust. York was a trading centre, and the artefacts come from far and wide: coins from Samarkand, a ceremonial axe-head made of amber from the Baltic, a cowrie shell from the Red Sea or the Persian Gulf.

One of the strangest discoveries was the world's largest known example of fossilised human dung – a mighty stool measuring all of 7 in (19.5 cm) long. The 'Lloyds Bank coprolite' contains hundreds of parasitic eggs, suggesting that the person who bequeathed it to us was riddled with intestinal worms.

The palaeoscatologist Andrew Jones, assessing its value for insurance purposes, described it 'the most exciting piece of excrement I've ever seen. In its own way it's as valuable as the Crown Jewels.' Unhappily, someone later dropped it, and the three pieces into which it broke had to be lovingly reassembled.

How the other half *lived*

How they *lived* in Coppergate

Life was tough for ordinary families in Viking York:

- People lived and worked cheek-by-jowl in houses typically measuring 22 x 16 ft (7 x 5 m) with wattle walls and thatched roofs.
- They were plagued by fleas and lice.
- Rubbish was thrown into the back yards, where a disgusting mish-mash of food remains, human waste and discarded building materials built up at the rate of about ⅜ inch (1 cm) a year.
- Their diet chiefly consisted of meat and bread. Local fish went off the menu when the rivers became polluted – and then they had to rely on fish brought in from the sea.

The word-hoard

The most obvious legacy of the Viking settlement can be read on the map and heard on the tongue. Yorkshire traditionally had its three Ridings (meaning literally 'thirds'), and although *wapentake* means nothing to most southerners, this word for the rough equivalent of the Saxon administrative 'hundred' is still used to signify an individual's home territory or sphere of influence.

Meanwhile, in Normandy

Renowned travellers, the Vikings foraged as far afield as North America, Russia and the Mediterranean.

The piratical Rollo was the French *bête noire* in the late 9th and early 10th centuries. King Charles the Simple finally bought him off with an offer of land.

This settlement of Norsemen became the duchy of Normandy, from which one of Rollo's descendants would later sail to claim the throne of England.

The former Danelaw is clustered with Scandinavian placenames. Here are a few of the most common endings:

-by	farmstead, village (*Grimsby*)
-dale	valley (*Nidderdale*)
-kirk	church (*Kirkby, Ormskirk*)
-ness	headland (*Furness*)
-thorpe	new village (*Scunthorpe*)
-thwaite	meadow (*Inglethwaite*)
-toft	small farmstead (*Lowestoft*)

So thoroughly have Scandinavian words invaded our vocabulary – some 2,000 of them in common usage – that we never give them a thought. Who would believe that those little words *they* and *their* displaced their former Anglo-Saxon equivalents?

Less known still is the effect of the Viking occupation on the very structure of our language. Old English had a complex series of inflections – variable word-endings to indicate grammatical meaning, as in Latin – but when Saxon traded with Dane these became a bar to understanding, and many of them fell away with no harm done at all.

And those 2,000 words? We'll make do with a mere 50:

awkward	outlaw
bag	race
billow	raft
birth	rake
bleak	ransack
both	root
bulk	rotten
cake	rugged
dirt	same
egg	scab
fellow	scant
gap	scare
gasp	score
guest	scowl
husband	scrub
hustings	shirt
ill	skill
knife	skin
law	skirt
leg	sky
loose	slaughter
mire	tight
muck	weak
muggy	window
odd	wrong

A forgotten man

Now's the time to introduce you to the most overlooked monarch in English history. If you've heard of Athelstan, who ruled from 924 to 939, you're in a very small minority – and yet he oversaw the flowering of a brief but glorious Anglo-Saxon renaissance before the Norsemen seized power again once and for all.

It wasn't all his own work. His father Edward the Elder, Alfred's son, had already begun to make inroads into the Danelaw, building fortresses as he advanced. There were still plenty of marauding Vikings about, as we shall see, but those who had settled in the country had become accustomed to a quieter life, and they were easier to overcome.

Athelstan finished that job, and in style. His decisive victory came at the Battle of Brunanburh in 937, after which – as an Old English poem recorded – 'five kings lay dead on the field'. Athelstan defeated the combined forces of the York, Welsh, Scots and Dublin Vikings. Wessex had unified the nation, and Athelstan was acclaimed king of England.

'From then on,' wrote the royal chronicler Aethelweard during a less happy time some 50 years later, 'the fields of Britain were consolidated into one, and there was peace and abundance of all things.'

The claim of British supremacy had a fleeting justification. It's said that after Brunanburh (probably in Cheshire), the kings of Cumbria, Wales, Strathclyde, Scotland and Wales rowed Athelstan along the River Dee in an act of homage.

The first royal portrait

Athelstan was the first Anglo-Saxon monarch to have his portrait painted, although he shares the scene with St Cuthbert, 'the wonder-worker of England'.

In his day-to-day life Athelstan wore his hair in ringlets braided with threads of gold, but in the painting (in a presentation copy of Bede's *Life of St Cuthbert*) he wears an imperial crown as he hands the haloed saint a book.

Athelstan – the first of our kings known not to have married – is buried at Malmesbury Abbey, Wiltshire.

But Athelstan's reputation rested on more than military conquest, great though that was. A pious man, he had his grandfather's love of learning and a similar organisational skill. The *Annals of Ulster* described him as 'the roof-tree of the dignity of the western world', while the 12th-century historian William of Malmesbury claimed that 'no one more just or more learned ever governed the kingdom'.

He wrote a line of self-criticism, which at the same time demonstrated his willingness to listen: 'I have learned that our peace is worse kept than I should like it, and my councillors say I have borne it for too long.'

- **He formulated a new code of laws, including strict rules on buying and selling.**

- **He attracted poets and scholars to his court and held national assemblies.**

- **He established a single currency for the entire kingdom.**

- **He married his half-sisters into the noble families of Europe to secure his throne – receiving in return illustrious gifts such as Constantine's sword and Charlemagne's lance.**

A saint's progress

We can chart the ups and downs of the next few English kings through the career of St Dunstan, who was born into a noble Wessex family around 910 and studied at Glastonbury Abbey under the Irish monks who occupied its ruins.

Thanks to his reputation as a scholar, musician and illuminator, Athelstan invited Dunstan to the court at Winchester, but he was banished after envious enemies intrigued against him – even beating him up and throwing him into a cesspool. He retired to Glastonbury, to live as a hermit.

During the reign of Athelstan's successor, **Edmund the Magnificent** (939–946), he was brought back to the court as a minister, and later became the abbot of Glastonbury, where he rebuilt the church and cloister and established Benedictine monasticism.

After Edmund was stabbed to death by an intruder, his brother **Eadred** (946–955) launched a policy of unification and conciliation with the Danish half of the kingdom. Dunstan was the king's right-hand man in a campaign to build more churches and reform both the clergy and the laity.

Eadred's death brought Edmund's son **Eadwig** (955–959) to the throne. Dunstan, having had the nerve to label Eadwig's future wife a strumpet, fled to the apparent sanctuary of his Glastonbury cloister, only for the king to set off in pursuit and plunder it. Dunstan fled to Flanders.

Eric Bloodaxe

Norse sagas paint Eric Bloodaxe as an all-conquering Viking warrior, but the reality was rather different. The heir to the throne of Norway, he gave it up to his younger brother without a fight. He came to England during the reign of Athelstan, and was perhaps created a sub-king to keep Northumbria under control.

After Athelstan's death he had some intermittent success in stirring the people of Northumbria into revolt, but his triumphs were brief. Even the Northumbrians seem to have tired of him, and he was killed in battle in 954.

Eadwig's reign was brief. His brother **Edgar the Peaceful** (959–975) was installed as king of the northern part of the kingdom after Mercia and Northumbria rose in revolt in 957, and within two years, on Eadwig's death, he unified the country once again. Dunstan was appointed archbishop of Canterbury. The coronation service which St Dunstan devised for Edgar still forms the basis of the ceremony performed in Westminster Abbey today.

When Edgar died there was a disputed succession. Dunstan plumped for the late king's eldest son **Edward** (975–978), while Edward's stepmother, Elfthryth, argued for her own son, Ethelred.

Tweaking the Devil's nose

Dunstan, legend has it, triumphed over the wiles of the Devil, who visited his forge at Glastonbury (Dunstan was a talented silversmith) in the guise of a beautiful young woman, hoping to seduce him. The saint, noticing a pair of cloven hoofs beneath his temptress's skirt, immediately seized the Devil's nose in the claws of his red-hot tongs.

Although Dunstan's faction won the day, civil war was in the air, and in March 978 Edward was assassinated at Corfe Castle in Dorset (and became henceforth St Edward the Martyr). Whether or not his mother had a hand in the murder, **Ethelred** (978–1016) now took shaky possession of the crown.

Dunstan's last public act was to conduct the coronation, and he seized the opportunity to condemn the bloody nature of the succession. 'Such evils shall come upon the English nation,' he predicted, 'as it has never suffered from since the time it came to England.' How prescient he was!

Danegeld

History knows the newly installed king as Ethelred the Unready – for which read 'ill-advised' or even 'witless' – because in his wretched reign the English raised the white flag of surrender. In his defence we should point out that he was only ten years old when he came to the throne and that he faced impossible odds in the shape of renewed Viking attacks both concerted and savage.

Here are a few lowlights from Ethelred's reign:

- In 991 the Vikings attacked Essex in no fewer than 80 ships. Ethelred responded by paying them huge amounts of blackmail money, known as *Danegeld* – and of course they kept coming back for more.

- The biggest payout of all came after Ethelred had ordered the St Brice's Day massacre (see page 97). Svein 'Forkbeard', incensed by the murder of his sister, exacted a sum reckoned to be worth four times the nation's income.

- In 1013 Ethelred fled to Normandy (where he married Emma, the duke's daughter).

- He returned the following year, on the death of Forkbeard – but only after the Witan (royal council) had made him promise to practise 'good government'.

1016 and *all* that

When Ethelred died in April 1016 his son, Edmund Ironside, continued English resistance to the forces of Forkbeard's son Canute (or Cnut), who had invaded the country with an army of some 20,000 men. After a series of battles the best Edmund could achieve was an agreement that he should keep Wessex, while Canute commanded every other part of the country.

It was a fruitless deal. Edmund died shortly afterwards, and Canute got the lot. Although Anglo-Saxon rule is commonly thought to have ended on what was to become the most famous date in English history, its demise actually occurred 50 years earlier, when – at Christmas 1016 – Canute was crowned king.

By the time he visited Rome for the coronation of the Holy Roman Emperor ten years later (his grandfather, Harald Bluetooth, had been the first Scandinavian king to accept Christianity), Canute rightfully claimed to be 'king of all England and Denmark and the Norwegians and some of the Swedes'.

Emma's boys

Early history doesn't give women much of a look-in, so let's here salute Emma (born around 985), the daughter of Richard the Fearless of Normandy, the second wife of Ethelred and, on his death, the second wife of Canute too. Two of her sons became king, one by each husband, and so did two of her stepsons (ditto) and her great-nephew, William the Conqueror.

Canute's death in 1035 sparked some family in-fighting, from which in 1040 Harthacnut (his son by Emma) emerged wearing the crown. When he died in the throes of an epileptic fit two years later, the wealthy Anglo-Danish courtier Godwin of Wessex stepped in to play power-broker.

Emma had had two sons by Ethelred, but one of them, Alfred, was no longer in the equation. Enemies of Harthacnut (who had sought to protect him) had captured Alfred, blinded him and inflicted such severe injuries that he died from his wounds soon afterwards.

That left Edward the Confessor, a 41-year-old celibate long since holed up safely in Normandy. He was now persuaded to return to England, marry Godwin's daughter and wear the crown. Even his mother had wanted it to be given to someone else.

Godwin's approval didn't last long. Once installed on the throne, Edward began, not surprisingly, to surround himself with friends and confidants from Normandy, where he'd lived for a quarter of a century.

fit for a king

Soon after coming to the throne in 1042, Edward the Confessor began rebuilding the Benedictine abbey of St Peter in London, founded by St Dunstan during the previous century. As Westminster Abbey it would become the venue for all royal coronations and burials.

The abbey was consecrated in 1065, a week before the Confessor's death. Some parts of his monastic dormitory survive in the Norman undercroft, but the only extant view of the original building is on the Bayeux Tapestry.

Sussex ports were granted to Fécamp Abbey across the Channel, the merchants of Rouen were given their own London port, Norman clerics were made English bishops, Norman magnates raised castles on newly gifted land, and court documents were written in French.

The Confessor – canonised a century later for his supposed, but barely demonstrated, piety – further stirred the pot by extending the role of his shire reeves, or king's sheriffs, so diminishing the influence of the Saxon nobles in their earldoms.

A sight for sore eyes

Leofric, earl of Mercia, may have been one of the most powerful nobles during the reign of Edward the Confessor, but his wife, Lady Godiva, has a fame which trumps his – even if the story is a little too good to be true.

It's said that she disapproved of the high taxes her husband was imposing on the people of Coventry, and made her protest by riding naked through the marketplace, her own assets hidden only by the length of her flowing locks.

In 1051 the disaffected Godwin was on the brink of civil war with the powerful Leofric, earl of Mercia, who supported Edward. Their two armies dispersed after wiser counsel prevailed, and Godwin was exiled until passions cooled.

When Godwin died in 1053, his son Harold succeeded him as Earl of Wessex – the richest and most powerful man in the country apart from Edward himself. He was biding his time.

The incumbent vs. the Bastard

Such was the tense situation as the Confessor lay on his deathbed in January 1066. Which faction should inherit the kingdom?

There were two chief candidates, each with arguments in his favour, neither with a clear-cut case.

- **Harold was the Confessor's brother-in-law, he received his last blessing (Edward handed over, just before he died, 'all the kingdom to your protection'), and he was the man chosen by the Witan – and crowned on 6 January.**

- **William, the son of the unmarried Duke of Normandy and his mistress, was easily dismissed as a bastard by his enemies (he is still sometimes called 'William the Bastard'), but he was a distant cousin of the Confessor, who he claimed had earlier promised him the crown. He also alleged that Harold, while in Normandy two years before, had sworn on a holy relic that William should be king – an unlikely story, but one told on that victor's version of events, the Bayeux Tapestry.**

The rest of the story is so well known that it needs only swift telling here. The Normans – another branch of the Viking family who had accepted Christianity generations before – had the Pope's backing for their invasion of England, and in September 1066 William set sail with an army of more than 10,000 men.

Harold performed heroics. First he had to deal with an attack in the north by the joint forces of his brother Tostig and Harald Hardrada, king of Norway. His troops defeated them (and killed both leaders) at Stamford Bridge in the East Riding of Yorkshire. They then had to march back south at speed to face William's army, which had landed at Pevensey on the Sussex coast.

The decisive battle was fought at an uninhabited spot some 6 miles (10 km) northwest of Hastings, where the Conqueror was later to build Battle Abbey and where the (helpfully signposted) battlefield can still be walked today.

It might easily have gone the other way, but William prevailed, Harold was killed – and so began a new era of English history.

A scene from the Bayeux Tapestry

A Domesday assessor makes his rounds

'Nothing can be said to be certain, except death and taxes.'

Benjamin Franklin

Chapter five

Feudal England

In the first days of 1086 the Conqueror's officials began appearing in towns, villages and hamlets the length and breadth of the kingdom, taking down details of fields, woods and pastures, who held them, the number of ploughs they used and how many pigs, sheeps and cows they kept.

Within a year William had in his hands the most detailed statistical record known to early European history. For the native English this tax collectors' bible smacked of Judgement Day – they called it the Domesday Book.

The *Anglo-Saxon Chronicle* gave it a damning review: 'There was not a single hide or rood of land nor, it is shameful to tell (but he thought it no shame to do), was there even an ox, cow or swine that was not set down in his writ.'

The *hide* was the basic unit of valuation. It had originally signified an area of land sufficient to sustain a household, but it had already lost that definition, and quite how the Domesday inquisitors assessed it is lost to us.

An entry from Oakley, Buckinghamshire: 'Aelfgyth the maid has half a hide which Godric the sheriff granted her as long as he was sheriff, on condition of her teaching his daughter gold embroidery work.'

The survey is an invaluable source for historians, packed as it is with population figures, occupations and working landscapes – 35 per cent was arable, 30 per cent pasture and 15 per cent woodland – but there are a few vexing gaps nevertheless. Churches, for instance, do make frequent appearances, but since the buildings had no economic relevance they are often ignored.

Much more important were mills (6,000 of them), fishponds, saltpans and the like. The point of the exercise, after all, was to name the landholders and assess how much revenue they could raise for the Crown.

William's commissioners, armed with a batch of set questions, arranged meetings with the local 'hundred'. Evidence was given under oath, and sometimes a second team of assessors was sent round to check on the findings of the first.

Devastation

One set of figures points unerringly to the cruelty of the invading army. Domesday records the value of a place in 1066 and again 20 years later, and there are often shocking discrepancies. After the great battle near Hastings, some of William's troops marched west to sack the Saxon treasury at Winchester, and the villages on their route were mercilessly ravaged and torched. The entry for Hurstpierpoint in West Sussex reads: 'Total value before 1066, £36; later £9; now £12 in all.'

The main body of the Norman army had marched on London by way of Dover and Canterbury. With London Bridge defended, the soldiers burned Southwark and went on a spree of rape and pillage through the surrounding countryside – areas recorded as 'waste' in the Domesday Book. A circle of fire was lit around London, whose citizens sued for peace.

Further afield there was continued, if sporadic, resistance. In 1069 an influx of Danes helped the local people retake York. Their success was brief and their punishment severe. The rapacious fury of William's response – the so-called 'Harrowing of the North' – wiped out the population between York and Durham, destroying their villages and burning their crops in the fields.

An estimated 100,000 people lost their lives through sword and famine. On his deathbed, it's said, the Conqueror remembered that 'I fell on the English of the northern shires like a ravening lion.' With an army of 12,000 to control a population of two or three million, he had opted for brute force and terror.

And then there was the great land-grab. Some 4,000 Saxons were forced to hand over their possessions to 200 Norman barons, bishops and abbots. (By 1086 only two bishops and three of the 21 barons were English.) The 12th-century chronicler Simeon of Durham reported that 'many men sold themselves into perpetual servitude, provided that they could maintain a certain miserable life'.

Hereward the Wake

We all like a valiant hero, and Hereward the Wake (a real person, albeit with Robin Hood-type myths attached) was a dispossessed Englishman who harried the Normans in the Cambridgeshire fens from his base on the Isle of Ely – a bolthole, too, for Earl Morcar of Northumbria and Bishop Ethelwine of Durham.

One chronicler tells us that when William's forces eventually took control of the island the rebels had their hands cut off and their eyes put out. Hereward, however, slipped away to continue his guerrilla activities – although what finally became of him we don't know.

The poor had few rights under this new regime. The draconian 'forest law' covered any land owned by the king, whether wooded or not – up to a third of the country eventually – and it came down severely on anyone caught poaching, with blinding the punishment for hunting a deer. Boars and hares were protected, and it wasn't enough to 'spare that tree' – you couldn't even gather firewood.

How the other half lived

How peasants were housed in Norman England

There wasn't much privacy for a poor family in those post-Conquest days. A typical house with a wooden frame, wattle-and-daub walls and a thatched roof had one room for eating and another for sleeping – and pigs and hens would often shuffle around in the straw on the trodden-earth floor, too.

There was no chimney, the smoke from the fire rising through open doors or narrow windows which would be shuttered against bad weather. And furniture? Little more than a trestle table, a bench, a few stools and a clothes chest.

High and low

The Normans didn't invent the feudal system – the Anglo-Saxons, after all, had always sworn fealty (loyalty) to their thegns (lords) – but its workings stand out in sharp relief during the period immediately after the Norman conquest.

Who owned England? The king – every last inch. And who 'held' it? A chain of people, for whom possession came with strict obligations:

- The barons, or tenants-in-chief, were given large tracts of land by the monarch, in return for which they pledged him military support.
- Next in line were the knights, lords of the manor to whom the nobles parcelled out land on the promise of recruiting men and gathering material for waging war.
- Below them were the villeins, freemen who paid their local lords in labour (so many hours a week) for the privilege of being given scattered strips of land to farm.
- And then there were serfs, or bondsmen – virtual slaves without any land at all – who did various lowly jobs in return for their keep.

Your guide to the Norman kings

• **William the Conqueror** (1066–1087)

He inherited the dukedom of Normandy in 1035 as a child, and later overcame rebellious barons to consolidate his power. After the Battle of Hastings he had to put down a series of rebellions in England, but by 1075 he felt secure enough to spend most of the rest of his reign back in Normandy. His eldest son, Robert, took up arms against him in France and was mollified only with the promise of the Normandy dukedom on his death.

• **William II** (1087–1100)

Better known as William Rufus, for his ruddy complexion and red hair, the Conqueror's second son was described by the *Anglo-Saxon Chronicle* as 'hateful to almost all his people and odious to God'. He fell out with the Church – seizing the revenues of Anselm, Archbishop of Canterbury, after forcing him into exile. He controlled his nobles in no-nonsense fashion, blinding and castrating one of them for alleged treason. William was killed by an arrow while hunting in the New Forest (the 'Rufus Stone' marks the supposed spot today), and the jury will always be out on whether this was an accident or murder.

• Henry I (1100–1135)

Rufus's younger brother was made of much better stuff. Known as 'Beauclerc' because of his learning, and 'the Lion of Justice' for his legal and administrative reforms – said to be the most sophisticated in Europe – he linked the rule of law to Anglo-Saxon tradition and granted the nobles a Charter of Liberties which has been seen as a forerunner of Magna Carta. He married a Scottish princess, symbolising a new accord between the Norman rulers and the conquered natives, and defeated his brother Robert to reunite England and Normandy. After the drowning of his 17-year-old son William in the *White Ship* disaster of 1120, Henry married his daughter Matilda to Geoffrey V of Anjou and named her as his successor in his will. He is said to have died of a surfeit of lampreys – an eel-like river fish.

• What happened next

The nobles broke their promise to accept Matilda as queen and instead supported the claim of Stephen of Blois, son of the Conqueror's daughter, Adela. Civil war (known as the Anarchy) continued until shortly before Stephen's death in 1154, with Matilda being the effective monarch – although not crowned as queen – for a few months in 1141. It was Matilda, however, who had the last word: her son Henry Plantagenet succeeded Stephen as king.

To the manor born

The English countryside was divided into more than 9,000 manors, each of them run by a lord – and there was often no neat fit between their boundaries and the existing hundreds. Just as a powerful lord might own several manors in different parts of the country, so areas of a village might be divided between two or more lordships. A man's duty was to his lord above anything else – and his happiness depended upon having either a fair or a cruel master.

Although Essex and Kent were exceptions, with small, square enclosed fields, in most of lowland England villagers shared large open fields divided into strips. Apart from giving the lord their due hours of labour, villeins were free to tend their own plots, which were scattered among those of their neighbours to ensure that everyone had a mixture of fertile and less productive soil.

Their other rights included turning out their animals onto the communal waste ground to feed, cutting hay from the meadow, and gathering fallen branches from local woodland for fuel or as building material.

There were two men you had to look out for:

- **The bailiff** was often an outsider, appointed by the lord of the manor to oversee his lands and buildings and to collect rents and fines.
- **The reeve** was a more constant presence: the local estate supervisor, who was on hand to make sure that nobody was shirking.

How the other half lived

Where our ancestors tilled

Most of the remaining open-field systems in England were enclosed during the 19th century, but there's a remarkable survivor in the village of Laxton, Nottinghamshire.

Here, three fields mentioned in a 1635 survey are still being worked by farmers who rely on the crops for their income. The strips each represented a day's ploughing in Norman times, and they've been broadened to suit modern farming techniques – but their purchase by the Crown Estate Commissioners has ensured their survival.

A building boom

If a new master was the most immediate evidence of the Conquest for an ordinary English farm labourer, a change to the physical landscape very soon materialised before his eyes, too. The Normans were great builders, and they imported the creamy-yellow Caen stone from their home territory to dress a plethora of formidable castles.

No sooner had he arrived than William guarded the Sussex coast he had just invaded with a castle at the rivermouth of each of the county's five (later six) administrative areas, known as 'rapes': Hastings, Pevensey, Lewes, Bramber and Arundel. By the Thames he raised the daunting Tower of London, and he planted yet more castles as his forces marched north to suppress the uprisings there.

The area bordering hostile Wales – the Marches – became almost an independent enclave, with trusted lords ruling the roost from Chester, Hereford and Shrewsbury and building a string of castles – among them Chepstow, Ludlow and Monmouth.

The Church was almost an equal partner with the Crown (the two would tussle for centuries), and these years saw the rebuilding of many parish churches in the round-arched Romanesque style. New churches were created, magnificent cathedrals soared to the heavens, and immensely rich monasteries and abbeys – sheep runs and all – spread across large tracts of countryside. The fact that much of their wealth was spirited away to mother houses in France would later be held against these so-called 'alien priories' populated by foreign monks.

A monastic meal

Christian soldiers

Many of the Norman rulers and their early successors were rugged individualists who saw no conflict between religious zeal, a lust for power and the brutal treatment of anyone who stood in their way. Throw in a dash of adventurous spirit – they loved the hunting field, after all – and it's easy to understand the appeal of the Crusades.

Their rationale was recovering the holy places in and around Jerusalem from the Muslim 'infidel'. Over a period of 200 years several hundreds of thousands of European soldiers took the long journey to the Holy Land.

- The **First Crusade** (1095–1091) was blessed by Pope Urban II. Robert of Normandy was among the Norman nobles who took Antioch in 1098 after a siege, and followed suit in Jerusalem the following year. On both occasions the inhabitants were massacred.

- In the **Second Crusade** (1147–1149) the Christian knights failed to retake Damascus, but joined forces with the Portuguese king Afonso I to capture Lisbon from the Moors. Among their numbers were members of the newly created religious military order the Knights Templar, wearing their distinctive uniform – a white mantle emblazoned with a large red cross.

- On hearing that combined Muslim forces under Saladin had overrun Crusader bases in 1187 and laid siege to Jerusalem, Pope Urban III suffered a fatal heart attack. His successor, Gregory VIII, immediately proposed the **Third Crusade** (1187–1192), enthusiastically taken up by three western rulers: the Holy Roman Emperor, Frederick Barbarossa (who died on the way), the English king Richard the Lionheart, and Philip II of France (who feigned illness in order to return home and capture Richard's Normandy duchy). Richard eventually negotiated a treaty with Saladin, allowing Christians access to the holy places.
- The **Fourth Crusade** (1202–1204) became sidetracked and sacked the Christian city of Constantinople, as religious power politics led to the 'great schism' between the Roman Catholic and Eastern Orthodox churches.

What happened next

The last official crusade was the ninth, from 1271 to 1272: it involved Edward I and was a failure. Other expeditions bearing the name were the Albigensian Crusade launched in 1209 to eliminate the heretical Cathars of southern France, and the Children's Crusade of 1212, which drew to its banner thousands of idealistic French and German teenagers and young people – and petered out in tragic failure.

The extensive ruins of the great Cistercian abbey of Fountains in north Yorkshire only hint at its stratospheric income. During its 13th-century heyday it farmed land in more than 200 parts of the north, including vast areas of Nidderdale; owned urban properties in York, Grimsby, Yarm, Boston and Scarborough; and had stakes in milling, fishing, horse-breeding, iron-smelting, mining and quarrying.

However devout the monks in their cloisters, this was big business with a spiritual face.

A tenth of everything

The massive tithe barns which survive in many parts of the country are a reminder of the days when villages had to deliver a tenth of their produce – corn, roots, milk, wool, even birds from their dovecotes – to the local church.

In times of drought and other hardships the tithe might occasionally be returned as a charitable donation, but this tax burden on the poor was usually rigorously enforced – and deeply resented.

Hooray for Henry

After almost twenty years of turmoil during which Stephen and Matilda had played out their bloody game of tug-of-war (see page 139), the nobles were ready for a strong king who would unite the nation. The man who stepped forward perfectly fitted the bill.

Henry, Count of Anjou, Matilda's son (and thus the Conqueror's great-grandson), was a handsome, red-haired, thick-set 21-year-old, a hardened warrior who had so turned the head of Eleanor of Aquitaine, ten years his senior, that she had divorced the king of France, Louis VII, in order to marry him. (She would bear him many children before their relationship turned dangerously sour.)

The knights who fought for Henry's Angevin empire wore a sprig of broom, or *planta genista*, on their helmets – and so, with the name anglicised, Henry II became the first in a long line of Plantagenet kings who would rule England for more than 300 years.

Two elements of a legal system he introduced to overcome the chaos of the Anarchy years are a lasting legacy of his reign.

- **Common law.** The existing ecclesiastical and civil courts had overlapping jurisdictions, and local nobles were in the habit of taking the law into their own hands. Henry's crackdown on crime involved imposing laws from the centre, with travelling justices visiting the shires to deal with both civil and criminal cases.

- **Trial by jury.** Being judged by your fellows wasn't new, but in 1179 juries were introduced to grand assizes to determine the guilt or otherwise of a defendant – although trial by ordeal and combat still continued.

A turbulent priest

In two other areas, however, Henry had far less success, and the first of these was his relationship with the Church. His biggest mistake was to appoint his chancellor and close bosom friend Thomas Becket as archbishop of Canterbury. Becket declined the post when it was first offered, presumably well aware of where acceptance would take their relationship. The king insisted, and

Becket immediately became a changed man – devout, prickly and dedicated to putting the Church first in everything.

Matters came to a head in 1164 with Henry's Constitutions of Clarendon, which stipulated (among other things) that clerics guilty of a crime should be tried in Crown rather than ecclesiastical courts. Becket refused to sign the document. After a Great Council convicted him of contempt of royal authority, he fled to the Continent and threatened Henry with excommunication.

After prolonged negotiations led to a kind of truce, Becket returned to England in 1170, only to infuriate the king all over again by excommunicating three of his supporters. Henry exploded in front of witnesses, asking 'Who will rid me of this turbulent priest?' (or words to that effect), whereupon four obliging knights rode to Canterbury and hacked Becket to death in front of the altar.

The archbishop had not been a popular man, but now he was a martyr – and Henry a religious pariah.

The shifting balance of power between Church and state (a national king having the armed might, but needing the blessing of a universal Pope) now swung so heavily against Henry that he was obliged to undertake three whole days of mourning, to agree that church courts be immune from royal interference, to promise that he would go on a crusade (he never did), to give land for new monasteries and to do penance at Canterbury by walking barefoot to Becket's shrine, stripping off and submitting himself to being whipped throughout the night by the monks.

Family matters

Henry also had trouble with his own flesh and blood. He alienated Eleanor in the traditional way, by enjoying a stream of mistresses, the most recent of whom was Rosamund Clifford. Eleanor, pregnant with her youngest son John when 'fair Rosamund' came on the scene in 1166, took herself off to the Angevin capital of Poitiers and proceeded to stir up as much trouble for him as she could. (Rosamund later retreated to a nunnery to die at the tender age of 26.)

And then there were his sons. In 1183 the oldest died in Aquitaine – Henry 'the Young King', who in 1170, at the age of 15, had been crowned joint monarch along with his father. That left Richard first in line to the throne, but Henry declined to nominate him because he preferred his younger brother John. Cue some mischief-making by Eleanor: Richard, despite itching to set off on the crusades, was persuaded to join the French king Philip II in attacking his own father's province of Anjou.

Troubadour love

Eleanor's grandfather William of Aquitaine is the earliest known troubadour poet, and she brought to her courts in England and France not only a devotion to poetry, music and the arts, but the code of 'courtly love'.

As sung by the minstrels, and idealised in the Arthurian romances of Geoffrey of Monmouth, this was a hothouse relationship between a man and a woman (never husband and wife), which blended spiritual yearning with unfulfilled sexual desire.

Worse was to follow. In 1189 John joined his brother in the revolt, at which news the failing Henry declared brokenly, 'I no longer care for anything in this world.'

It's not difficult to understand why Henry distrusted Richard. The 'Lionheart' was no sooner on the throne than he released his father's enemies from prison, brought his mother Eleanor back from France and burdened the people with crippling taxes in order to finance his obsession with the Crusades. He left for Palestine within a year, would return to England only once, and died of blood poisoning during a siege in France, after a crossbow wound turned septic.

King John and Magna Carta

But his brother John was no better, and the country was soon in chaos again. He fell out with the Pope (and, abjectly, had to offer England as a fiefdom of the papacy for his sins), was impotent as the Welsh overran his Marcher castles, faced armed rebellion from his barons and retreated to the Tower of London as armed mobs roamed the streets.

The upshot was his enforced signature to a document whose limitations on the power of the monarchy have reverberated down the ages. Magna Carta was, of course, no democratic manifesto – and John swiftly had his new friend the Pope annul it – but its spirit would never die. Here's clause 39:

> No free man shall be arrested or imprisoned or deprived or outlawed or exiled or in any way ruined . . . except by lawful judgment of his peers or by the law of the land.

Citizen power

Towns grew steadily during the medieval period, and once they were granted a charter by the king they were allowed to conduct their own affairs without interference from local nobles.

London was the most prosperous commercial centre and produced large revenues for the monarch, but Richard's imposition of extra taxes to pay for the Crusades provoked the citizens to form a 'commune' to protect their interests. They elected Henry Fitz-Ailwyn as their leader – the very first mayor of London.

Your handy guide to the *first ten Plantagenets*

Henry II (reigned 1154–1189)
A reforming monarch who united the nation but left it to incompetent offspring.

Richard I (1189–1199)
More interested in the Crusades than in his kingdom, which he taxed heavily and used as a cash cow.

John (1199–1216)
Weak, and forced to sign Magna Carta.

Henry III (1216–1272)
He angered the English church by granting a fifth of its income to the Pope, and the barons by favouring the French relatives of his wife, Eleanor of Provence. His defeat by Simon de Montfort led to the first parliament – although it didn't last.

Edward I (1272–1307)
Henry's giant of a son ('Longshanks') created a series of statutes which became the first body of English laws based on Magna Carta. He brutally attacked the Welsh, and then turned north to become 'the Hammer of the Scots'. In 1290 he expelled all Jews from England, and they would not be allowed to return for more than 350 years.

Edward II (1307–1327)
Edward I's son was a disaster. His wife Isabella (ignored while he dallied with his 'favourite' Piers Gaveston) joined forces with Roger Mortimer to overthrow him in favour of their 14-year-old son.

Edward III (1327–1377)
He banished his domineering mother and had Mortimer executed. A brilliant general, he launched the Hundred Years' War with France. His son, the Black Prince, would have inherited the crown, but he died first.

Richard II (1377–1399)
The Black Prince's son survived the Peasants' Revolt but not the rebellion of his cousin, and childhood playmate, Henry Bolingbroke.

Henry IV (1399–1413)
Having taken the crown by force, he spent his reign putting down rebellions.

Henry V (1413–1422)
Vigorously pursued the war with France. At home he was generally fair, but ruthless in putting down the Lollards (see page 162), having his riotous friend Sir John Oldcastle (Shakespeare's Falstaff) burned to death.

What happened next
There were still four Plantagenet kings to come, the last (Richard III) falling at Bosworth Field.

The barons were so incensed by John's back-pedalling that they invited the French prince Louis to replace him. John fled to East Anglia (losing the crown jewels as he crossed the Wash in haste), and in May 1216 Louis duly arrived in London to be proclaimed – though not yet anointed – king of England.

Who knows how history might have turned out had John not promptly died? Now the guardians of his 9-year-old son Henry rushed him to Gloucester Abbey, where he was crowned with a circlet of gold. He would reign (as Henry III) for all of 56 years.

Simon says

Henry had his own Magna Carta moment after being defeated by the nobles under Simon de Montfort at the Battle of Lewes in 1264. What followed was the nation's first taste of parliamentary rule, each shire represented by two knights and each town by two burgesses.

It didn't last (Simon de Montfort was killed the following year) but, like Magna Carta, it set an unforgotten precedent.

And yet kings are only a part of our story. The common man and woman would generally observe their doings from a distance, although taking a greater interest when – in the form of ravaging armies, visiting justices, cathedral building – their policies affected life closer to home.

What, one wonders, did they make of the constant to-and-fro of each post-Conquest monarch between his English realm and his possessions across the Channel? How much did they care about the long-drawn-out conflict with France which Henry's successors indulged in for almost a hundred years?

It's safe to say that nothing affected them as deeply as an invasion which those knights in armour were powerless to prevent – an army of engorged fleas hitching a ride on the backs of black rats.

The war of the flea: a small but deadly menace devastates the land

Chapter Six

TROUBLES GALORE

The Black Death came ashore on the south coast of England in the summer of 1348, and within a little more than a year it had the whole country in its ghastly grip. At least a third of the population – possibly more than half – was wiped out by a disease which left its stricken victims in a delirium and vomiting blood, their flesh brocaded with eruptions of infected black swellings, or buboes.

They knew it variously as the 'murrain', the 'pestilence' and the 'great mortality'.

Illiterate rural peasants – some 90 per cent of the population – could leave us no record of their agonies, but contemporary accounts by the clergy reveal the horror.

> Alas for our sorrow! This mortality swept away so vast a multitude of both sexes that none could be found to carry the corpses to the grave. Men and women bore their own offspring on their shoulders to the church and cast them into a common pit. From these there proceeded so great a stench that hardly anyone dared to cross the cemeteries.
>
> William Dene, a monk at Rochester, Kent

The enclosed nature of monasteries made them a fertile breeding ground for the deadly bacteria (monks, canons and lay brothers succumbed in large numbers), while the overcrowded and insanitary conditions in the towns presented them with an open invitation. Excavations of cemeteries in the Smithfield area of London have revealed bodies stacked five deep. Three archbishops of Canterbury died in quick succession, and the abbot of Westminster and 27 of his monks were buried at the abbey.

The bolshie brigade

A cold winter at last checked the disease – and the survivors who emerged blinking into the bright days of spring 1351 suddenly found themselves in a new England altogether.

Something had changed in the temper of the downtrodden. As land lay untilled and animals untended, they found that their labour now had a greater value – in some cases a cash value for the first time – and they were determined to profit from it. The lord of the manor certainly wasn't going to harness himself to the plough or tote bags of wheat to the mill. If he refused to pay his underlings extra, they would simply go and find work in the fields of another man whose bailiff asked no questions.

The authorities jumped on this as severely as they could. Edward III, responding to the pleas of the land-owning class, published his Statute of Labourers in 1351. It condemned 'the malice of employees, who were idle and were not willing to take employment after the pestilence unless for outrageous wages'.

An English Bible

The turbulent iconoclasm of the 14th century found religious expression in the life and work of the Yorkshire-born theologian John Wycliffe (c.1320–1384), a forerunner of the Protestant reformer Martin Luther. Their enemies called his uneducated followers 'Lollards' (possibly meaning 'babblers' or 'mumblers') – and the name stuck.

In 1381 Wycliffe was dismissed from the University of Oxford for his attack on the Church and the monasteries. Among the practices he opposed were:

- **prayers for the dead in chantries**
- **confessions to priests**
- **icons in churches**
- **clerical celibacy**
- **exorcism.**

Believing that authority over matters of Christian belief lay in the Scriptures rather than in the Church of Rome, he translated the Bible from the Latin Vulgate into English for the use of the minority of ordinary believers then able to read.

The first version of Wycliffe's Bible was completed in 1384. The church swiftly attempted to suppress it, but without success – more than 250 copies survive.

The statute laid down a harsh set of rules to force labourers back under the cosh.

- **All men and women were obliged to take the work they had in 1346 'or five or six years earlier', and for the same wages.**
- **If they refused, they were to be punished by imprisonment.**

This worked only patchily because the economic realities were too powerful, but the authorities still failed to read the signs. In 1380, wanting more cash for the French wars, Parliament imposed a 'poll tax' (three groats per head) which fell equally on rich and poor, men and women – and the anger of the people welled up into a gathering tide of protest.

The Peasants' Revolt, then known as the Great Rising, was preached by the Lollard priest John Ball. His mentor John Wycliffe (see facing page) was opposed to the insurrection, but Ball wrapped religious and political radicalism in one package. 'When Adam delved and Eve span,' he famously rhymed in one of his sermons, 'who was then the gentleman?'

Under the leadership of Wat Tyler and Jack Straw, an army of some 50,000 – not only peasants, but 'respectable' leaders of village life – marched on London on 14 June 1381. Some of them forced their way into the Tower and beheaded Robert de Hales, the Lord Treasurer, and Simon of Sudbury, who was both Lord Chancellor and Archbishop of Canterbury. The hated financier Richard Lyons was caught elsewhere in the city, and similarly dispatched. (The executed Lord Chancellor's part-mummified head, axe mark and all, is on display at St Gregory's church in his native Sudbury, Suffok.)

Their blood up, the rebels destroyed John of Gaunt's Savoy Palace and obliged the king – Gaunt's nephew, the 14-year-old Richard II – to address their grievances.

At Smithfield the next day the scene was set for a decisive confrontation. Tyler spurred his horse forward to discuss terms with the boy monarch, surrounded by his advisers. The rebels' demands included the sacking of unpopular ministers and the abolition of serfdom. It seemed that Richard would have little choice but to agree – until the Lord Mayor of London, Sir William Walworth, hacked at Tyler's neck with his sword and Sir John Cavendish followed up by running the rebel leader through.

At this crucial moment Richard called to the outraged crowd 'You shall have no captain but me,' and promised that all their demands would be met. He of course backtracked on all of this once the rebel army had dispersed, and many of its leaders (including John Ball) were pursued, captured and executed. But it had been a very close-run thing.

Lingua franca

And how, during this tempestuous period, was the native speech of Wat Tyler and his cohorts coping with the flowery tongue of the Plantagenet master race? Very well, thank you! The two had fused into what we now call Middle English, a richly expressive language with French embellishments grafted onto a resistant Anglo-Saxon grammatical structure. However far apart kings and rebels might still be, their language spoke of assimilation.

Nothing more urgently accelerates the need for successful communication than the heat of sexual desire. For many Normans the Englishwomen were sleeping dictionaries.

Henry Hitchings, *The Secret Life of Words*

Of around 27,000 words first written down in this period, more than a fifth were French in origin, and many reflected such imported refinements as chivalry, hunting and cookery.

Yet these additions were merely parts of a new amalgam, and the late 14th century witnessed what some linguists have acclaimed 'the triumph of English' – a common language spoken, we might add, by a people who now had even their first names in common. It was farewell to Frideswide and Morcar at the font; welcome to little Elizabeth and William.

- **In 1362 the Statute of Pleading ruled that English, rather than French, should be the oral language of courts and of Parliament.**
- **Leading by example, Edward III gave his opening speech to Parliament in English that year – the first time it had ever been done.**
- **In 1399 Henry IV made the first coronation address in English.**

Three masterpieces

But we shouldn't imagine that the language was any more fixed than the turbulent society which used it. Three major works which have come down to us from those closing years of the 14th century demonstrate sharp divisions in both literary conventions and contemporary lifestyles.

In ***Piers Plowman***, William Langland has the humble labourer of his title set out to track down the characters Dowel (Do-Well), Dobet (Do-Better) and Dobest (Do-Best) in order to discover how to live a true Christian life. Although Langland uses traditional unrhymed alliterative verse, his style has nothing of the brash vigour and bloody confrontation of the much earlier *Beowulf* poet. What he gives us instead, in simple plain man's language, are religous allegory and social satire – and he doesn't pull his punches.

He begins with a vision in which 'a fair field full of folk' lies between a hilltop tower and a dungeon in a deep valley (symbols of heaven and hell). We soon get to meet those 'folk'.

How the masses were entertained

The wonderful street theatre known as 'mystery' plays gave an illiterate community a much more colourful and rumbustious interpretation of the major events in the Christian calendar – from the Creation to the Day of Judgement – than they could ever hope to pick up in the churches with their ritualised Latin masses.

The heyday of the mystery plays lasted from the 14th century to the 16th. They were performed in English, and in their mixing of comic scenes with profound matters of life and death they influenced (think of the drunken porter scene in *Macbeth*) the later Elizabethan and Jacobean playwrights.

Originally much more tepid affairs put on inside the churches, they soon escaped into the marketplaces of the towns, where the craft guilds would compete to put on the most lavish or the most dramatic performances.

The individual plays formed parts of a cycle, and in their medieval heyday casts of travelling amateur and professional actors would perform for up to 20 hours at a time on festival days, strutting their stuff on decorated carts above the crowds.

As many as 48 pageants survive from York, 32 from Wakefield (the Towneley cycle) and 24 from Chester.

Although some of those who took part in the 1381 rebellion drew on the poem for their inspiration, they had to be selective. Piers may be dismissive of corrupt churchmen, but when he moves among the peasants he is equally angered by their ready excuses not to work. 'If anyone is truly blind or crippled, or has his limbs bolted with irons,' he says in Christlike fashion, 'he shall eat wheaten bread and drink at my table until God in his goodness brings him better days. But as for you – you could work for Truth well enough if you wanted to.'

In ***Sir Gawain and the Green Knight*** (by an unknown poet) we move away from the real world of post-Black Death England into the glittering fantasy land of Arthurian legend. If you consider the contrast improbable, take a brief glimpse inside the court of Edward III. He was, indeed, a genuine warrior, but there was nothing he enjoyed better than arranging Round Table events at Windsor Castle (he had a building especially constructed for them, larger than the Pantheon in Rome), during which he, his queen and their courtiers dressed in romantic gear and watched jousting tournaments.

The poem is alliterative, but brilliant in its imagery where Langland is homely. A massive knight dressed all in green challenges one of Arthur's knights to strike him with an axe on condition that he return the visit in a year and a day. Sir Gawain takes a swing, and the green knight's head flies off – whereupon he gathers it up and sets off for home. The rest of the poem recounts Gawain's adventures as he sets out to keep his promise, facing fierce challenges to his bravery and knightly fidelity.

And then there's Geoffrey Chaucer. In ***The Canterbury Tales*** we meet a large range of characters from middle England – not the peasants in Langland's 'fair field full of folk' and not the nobility (although Chaucer knew them well), but a publican, a miller, a clerk, a wife of Bath who is not as good as she ought to be, a summoner (court official), a pardoner (seller of indulgences) and so on.

Reading this sophisticated, allusive rhymed verse, drawing on French and Italian influences rather than the alliterative tradition, don't we persuade ourselves that all 14th-century life is here?

A hundred years of fratricide

For the Plantagenets, however, there was a world beyond England – and it was a world that would draw them back across the Channel for generations. In 1337 Philip VI of France seized Edward III's duchy of Aquitaine, and Edward responded by renewing an earlier claim to the French throne. (Suffice it to say that there had been dynastic complications.)

So began the so-called Hundred Years' War, which is usually reckoned to have continued, with comfort breaks, until 1453. We can see it as a conflict between close relatives – and, for any benighted English peasant who had suffered first poverty, then the Black Death and finally taxation to pay for continual warfare, a bitter them-and-us attitude towards their divided English/French royalty was surely inevitable.

It's unclear whether Edward believed he could ever win an outright victory, but there's no doubt that he enjoyed giving the French a bloody nose as often as he could. His tactic was to mount expeditions known as *chevauchées* – large-scale, speedy raids deep into French territory, with systematic plundering and the burning of buildings and crops in the field.

- **In 1346 Edward won the Battle of Crécy and then took control of Calais to give the English a major port on the Channel coast.**

- **Ten years later his son, the Black Prince, defeated the then French king, John II, at Poitiers and took him prisoner.**

- **In 1359 Edward was back again, now attempting to take Reims. This time he failed. A subsequent treaty gave him a huge ransom for the return of King John and an enlarged Aquitaine independent of the French crown – but on condition that he would renounce his claim to the French throne.**

Edward did eventually change his mind about that, but the French would be spared further serious aggravation until Henry V began to flex his muscles in 1415.

At the Battle of Agincourt, won by the English longbow against superior odds, we witness the Plantagenets in their pomp:

This day is called the feast of Crispian:
He that outlives this day, and comes safe home,
Will stand a tiptoe when the day is named,
And rouse him at the name of Crispian.

And gentlemen in England now abed
Shall think themselves accursed they were
not here,
And hold their manhoods cheap whiles any
speaks
That fought with us upon Saint Crispin's day.

– words not actually spoken by Henry, of course, but gloriously put into his mouth by a man who stands in the wings, awaiting his cue to step onto the stage in our next volume…

The Agincourt Carol

This rousing song for three voices may have been composed soon after the victory at Agincourt in 1415. Both poet and composer are anonymous. Spelling has been modernised.

Deo gratias, Anglia, redde pro victoria![1]

Our king went forth to Normandy
with grace and might of chivalry.[2]
There God for him wrought marvellously,
wherefore England may call and cry,

Deo gratias![3]

He set a siege, the sooth[4] for to say,
to Harflu[5] town with royal array.
That town he won, and made affray
that France shall rue till Doomesday.

Deo gratias!

...

Then, forsooth, that knight comely
in Agincourt field he fought manly.
Through grace of God most mighty
he had both the field and the victory.

Deo gratias!

...

1. Give thanks to God, England, for the victory. *2. cavalry*
3. Thanks be to God. *4. truth* *5. Honfleur*

Now gracious God He save our king,
his people and all his well-willing.[6]
Give him good life and good ending,
that we with mirth may safely sing,

Deo gratias!

6. those who wish him well

A 15th-century recipe

Beef y-Stywyd (Stewed Beef)

Take fayre beef of the rybbys of the fore quarterys, an smyte in fayre pecys, an wasche the beef in-to a fayre potte; than take the water that the beef was sothin yn, an strayne it thorw a straynowr, an sethe[1] the same water and beef in a potte, an let hem boyle to-gederys;[2] than take canel, clowes, maces, graynys of parise, quibibes,[3] and oynons y-mynced, perceli, an sawge, an caste ther-to, an let hem boyle to-gederys; an than take a lof of brede, an stepe it with brothe an venegre, an than draw it thorw a straynoure, and let it be stylle; an whan it is nere y-now,[4] caste the lycour ther-to, but nowt to moche, an than let boyle onys, an cast safroun ther-to a quantyte; than take salt an venegre, and cast ther-to, an loke that it be poynaunt[5] y-now, and serue forth.

1. boil 2. together 3. For these ingredients, see the modern version overleaf. 4. enough 5. pungent, spicy

Modern version

Ingredients:

- 1 lb (450 g) beef (fore quarter)
- 2–3 onions, chopped
- small loaf of bread, broken into pieces
- vinegar to taste
- herbs and spices to taste: cinnamon, cloves, mace, Guinea pepper ('grains of paradise'), Java pepper, parsley, sage, saffron, salt

Method:

1. Cut the beef into pieces, bring to the boil and simmer until tender.
2. Strain the water, then put the beef and water back into the pot. Add the onion, cinnamon, cloves, mace, peppers, parsley and sage, and bring back to the boil.
3. Take some of the broth and soak the bread in it; add vinegar.
4. When thoroughly steeped, strain the liquid and let it stand.
5. When the beef is ready, pour some of this liquid into the pot, but not too much. Bring to the boil once more. Add saffron and salt, and more vinegar if required.
6. Taste for spiciness, then serve.

Royal reigns

Kings and queens of England

• House of Wessex
802–839 Egbert
839–858 Ethelwulf
858–860 Ethelbald
860–865 Ethelbert
865–871 Ethelred
871–899 Alfred the Great
899–924 Edward the Elder
924–939 Athelstan
939–946 Edmund
946–955 Eadred
955–959 Eadwig
959–975 Edgar
975–978 St Edward the Martyr
978–1013 Ethelred the Unready

• House of Denmark
1013–1014 Sweyn Forkbeard

• House of Wessex
1014–1016 Ethelred the Unready (again)
1016 Edmund Ironside

• House of Denmark
1016–1035 Canute (Cnut)
1035–1040 Harold Harefoot
1040–1042 Harthacnut

• House of Wessex
1042–1066 St Edward the Confessor
1066 Harold

• House of Normandy
1066–1087 William I, the Conqueror
1087–1100 William II
1100–1135 Henry I
1135–1154 Stephen (disputed with Matilda, in power 1141)

• House of Plantagenet
1154–1189 Henry II
1189–1199 Richard I, the Lionheart
1199–1216 John
1216–1272 Henry III
1272–1307 Edward I
1307–1327 Edward II
1327–1377 Edward III
1377–1399 Richard II

• House of Lancaster
1399–1413 Henry IV
1413–1422 Henry V
1422–1461 Henry VI

• House of York
1461–1470 Edward IV

• **House of Lancaster**
1470–1471 Henry VI (again)

• **House of York**
1471–1483 Edward IV (again)
1483 Edward V
1483–1485 Richard III

• **House of Tudor**
1485–1509 Henry VII
1509–1547 Henry VIII
1547–1553 Edward VI
1553 Jane Grey (disputed)
1553–1558 Mary I
1558–1603 Elizabeth I

• **House of Stuart**
1603–1625 James I of England and VI of Scotland
1625–1649 Charles I

• **Commonwealth and Protectorate**
1649–1660 no ruling monarch

• **House of Stuart**
1660–1685 Charles II
1685–1688 James II of England and VII of Scotland
1689–1702 William III, co-ruler with:
1689–1694 Mary II
1702–1707 Anne

Kings and queens of the United Kingdom

• **House of Stuart**
1707–1714 Anne

• **House of Hanover**
1714–1727 George I
1727–1760 George II
1760–1820 George III
1820–1830 George IV
1830–1837 William IV
1837–1901 Victoria

• **House of Wettin (Saxe-Coburg-Gotha)**
1901–1910 Edward VII

• **House of Windsor**
1910–1936 George V
1936 Edward VIII
1936–1952 George VI
1952–present Elizabeth II

Glossary

alien priories Medieval religious houses which owed their allegiance to mother foundations in France.

barrow (see **tumulus**)

berserkers Viking soldiers renowned for their ferocity.

blood eagle A grim Viking torture, the lungs being torn from a living victim.

bloomery An ancient Roman ironworking site.

Brythonic One of two branches of the Celtic language spoken in Britain, the other (chiefly in Scotland and Ireland) being Goidelic.

burh A Saxon fortified town.

causewayed enclosure A prehistoric site, purpose unknown, its central area surrounded by concentric ditches crossed by a series of causeways.

chantry An altar or chapel where prayers were said for the dead.

chevauchée A lightning attack by the English in French territory during the Hundred Years' War.

colonia A Roman settlement for retired soldiers.

coppicing The cutting back of tree stools on a regular basis in order to produce strong, narrow shoots for fencing, charcoal, etc.

cross dyke A prehistoric landscape feature, consisting of a linear earthwork running across a ridge or the neck of a spur.

Danegeld Bribes given by Anglo-Saxons to keep the Vikings at bay.

Danelaw The large area of northeastern England granted to the Viking invaders as part of a treaty with the Saxons.

dendrochronology The study of tree rings as a guide to dating timber structures.

DNA Deoxyribonucleic acid, which contains the genetic instructions for the development of living organisms. It can be used to trace our genetic origins.

Domesday Book The Saxon name for the detailed Norman record of landholdings for tax purposes.

dyke An ancient earthwork raised as a boundary marker or defensive barrier.

feudal system A hierarchy, based on land ownership, in which each stratum of society owes obligations to the one above.

Five Boroughs A group of Midland towns (Leicester, Lincoln, Nottingham, Derby and Stamford) forming part of the Danelaw.

futhork The Anglo-Saxon version of the runic alphabet.

Harrowing of the North The brutal suppression of revolt in northern England after the Norman Conquest.

henge A neolithic earthwork with a ring bank and ditch, often containing circles of stone or timber.

Heptarchy The seven major kingdoms of Anglo-Saxon England.

hide The basic unit of valuation used in the Domesday Book, initially denoting an area of land capable of sustaining a single household.

hundred An administrative area of Anglo-Saxon England, originally supporting roughly 100 families.

kenning A formulaic phrase in Anglo-Saxon poetry, such as *bone-house* for 'body'.

knapping The striking of a piece of flint in order to provide sharp edges for a tool or weapon.

Lollard A follower of religious reformer John Wycliffe.

longships Speedy boats with a shallow draft used to carry Viking soldiers and traders.

manor A medieval estate ruled by a lord, to whom the locals owed various duties.

Marcher lords Powerful nobles given special privileges

by the king after the Norman conquest in return for controlling the border, or 'Marches', with Wales.

moot In Anglo-Saxon England, a meeting of the prominent men in a locality.

open fields A medieval agricultural system, with strips of farming land divided among local families.

palaeoscatologist A scientist who studies ancient dung.

paterae Metal urns used by the Romans at Bath to make offerings of holy water.

prehistory The period in a culture before written records.

rape One of six administrative areas into which the Normans divided the county of Sussex.

runes An ancient Germanic form of writing, most often found on inscriptions.

Saxon Shore Coastal defences raised by the Romano-Britons against raids by Saxon pirates.

sceatta A small silver coin – the first common currency of Anglo-Saxon England.

serf A member of the lowest feudal class in Norman England: a virtual slave.

tithe barn A very large barn in which a rector stored his 10% dues of produce from local farmers.

tor enclosure A prehistoric feature of hilltops in the southwest of England, in which stone walls enclose natural rock outcrops.

tumulus (plural **tumuli**) A prehistoric burial mound.

vallum A Roman rampart flanked by an outer ditch.

villein In feudal times, a tenant farmer legally tied to a lord of the manor.

wapentake A northern word, from the Scandinavian, referring to one's home territory or sphere of influence.

weregild The compensation granted to the victim of a crime in Anglo-Saxon times.

Witan (or **Witenagemot**) An assembly of the ruling class in Anglo-Saxon England.

An early England timeline

15,000 BC First men and women arrive in England following the last Ice Age.

6000 BC Mesolithic period. Rising sea level separates England from the Continent. England populated by hunter-gatherers.

4500 BC Neolithic period. First farmers.

3100 BC First ditch and bank constructed at Stonehenge.

2100–700 BC Bronze Age.

2000 BC Beaker Folk pottery appears.

700 BC Iron Age.

55 and 54 BC Roman general (subsequently dictator) Julius Caesar leads expeditions to Britain.

AD 43 Roman invasion under Emperor Claudius.

60–61 Boudica (Boadicea) of the Iceni tribe leads a revolt against the Romans.

128 Hadrian's Wall completed between the River Tyne and the Solway Firth.

142 Antonine Wall built between the rivers Forth and the Clyde.

287 Carausius, commander of the Romans' British Fleet, begins Saxon Shore defences and declares himself emperor of Britain and northern Gaul.

367 Saxons, Picts and Scots break through Hadrian's wall and kill the Count of the Saxon Shore.

410 The Romans withdraw their legions from Britain.

577 Battle of Deorham (near Gloucester) establishes border between Celts and Saxons in the West Country.

597 St Augustine converts the people of Kent to Christianity.

664 Synod of Whitby, at which Oswiu of Northumbria chooses the Roman form of Christianity over the Celtic.

681 Sussex, converted by St Wilfrid, is the last English county to accept Christianity.

787 First death at the hands of the Vikings.

793 Vikings sack the monastery on Lindisfarne (Holy Island).

869 Martyrdom of St Edmund.

871 Alfred becomes king of Wessex.

878 Battle of Ethandun (probably Edington, Wiltshire): Alfred defeats the Danes under Guthrum and their treaty establishes the Danelaw.

937 Battle of Brunanburh (location uncertain), after which Athelstan is acclaimed king of England.

960 St Dunstan becomes Archbishop of Canterbury.

978 Murder of King Edward 'the Martyr'.

991 Battle of Maldon, Essex. Ethelred 'the Unready' pays Danegeld.

1002 St Brice's Day Massacre of Danes.

1016 Canute becomes first Viking king of England.

1042 Edward the Confessor begins to build Westminster Abbey.

1066 King Harold defeats Harald Hardrada at the Battle of Stamford Bridge, but loses to William the Conqueror at Hastings.

1069–1070 'Harrowing of the North' by Norman forces.

1086 Domesday Book compiled.

1095 Start of the First Crusade.

1100 William Rufus killed by an arrow in the New Forest.

1120 Heir to the throne Prince William is drowned in the *White Ship* disaster.

1135–1154 'The Anarchy' – civil war between Stephen and Matilda, rival claimants to the English throne.

1170 Martyrdom of Thomas Becket at Canterbury.

1215 King John agrees to sign Magna Carta, limiting the power of the monarchy.

1264 Henry III agrees to parliamentary rule after defeat by Simon de Montfort at the Battle of Lewes, East Sussex.

1290 Edward I expels Jews from England.

1337–1453 Hundred Years' War between England and France.

1346 English victory at Battle of Crécy.

1348 Black Death arrives in England.

1351 Edward III issues Statute of Labourers to keep wages low.

1356 English victory at Battle of Poitiers.

1362 Statute of Pleading makes English the oral language of the courts and Parliament.

1381 Peasants' Revolt.

1384 Publication of John Wycliffe's Bible in English.

1415 English victory at Battle of Agincourt (present-day Azincourt, northeast France).

Index

Other volumes in this set:

England: A Very Peculiar History

Volume 2: From the Wars of the Roses to the Industrial Revolution

by Ian Graham ISBN: 978-1-908973-38-2

Volume 3: From Trafalgar to the New Elizabethans

by John Malam ISBN: 978-1-908973-39-9

The Cherished Library

Edited by Stephen Haynes

A CLASSIFIED LIST
OF THE FIRST 43 VOLUMES

Available in hardback binding
and for all digital platforms

Very Peculiar Histories™

History of the British Isles

England (in 3 volumes)

Vol. 1: From Ancient Times to Agincourt *David Arscott* 978-1-908973-37-5

Vol. 2: From the Wars of the Roses to the Industrial Revolution *Ian Graham* 978-1-908973-38-2

Vol. 3: From Trafalgar to the New Elizabethans *John Malam* 978-1-908973-39-9

Boxed set of all three volumes: 978-1-908973-41-2

Scotland (in 2 volumes) *Fiona Macdonald*

Vol. 1: From Ancient Times to Robert the Bruce 978-1-906370-91-6

Vol. 2: From the Stewarts to Modern Scotland 978-1-906714-79-6

Ireland *Jim Pipe* 978-1-905638-98-7

Wales *Rupert Matthews* 978-1-907184-19-2

History of the 20th century

Titanic *Jim Pipe* 978-1-907184-87-1

World War One *Jim Pipe* 978-1-908177-00-1

World War Two *Jim Pipe* 978-1-908177-97-1

The Blitz *David Arscott* 978-1-907184-18-5

Rations *David Arscott* 978-1-907184-25-3

The 60s *David Arscott* 978-1-908177-92-6

Social history

Victorian Servants *Fiona Macdonald* 978-1-907184-49-9

North of the Border

Scottish Clans *Fiona Macdonald* 978-1-908759-90-0

Scottish Tartan and Highland Dress *Fiona Macdonald* 978-1-908759-89-4

Scottish Words *Fiona Macdonald* 978-1-908759-63-4

Whisky *Fiona Macdonald* 978-1-907184-76-5

British places

Brighton *David Arscott* 978-1-906714-89-5

London *Jim Pipe* 978-1-907184-26-0

Yorkshire *John Malam* 978-1-907184-57-4

Famous Britons

Great Britons *Ian Graham*	978-1-907184-59-8
Robert Burns *Fiona Macdonald*	978-1-908177-71-1
Charles Dickens *Fiona Macdonald*	978-1-908177-15-5
William Shakespeare *Jacqueline Morley*	978-1-908177-15-5

Sports and pastimes

Cricket *Jim Pipe*	978-1-908177-90-2
Fishing *Rob Beattie*	978-1-908177-91-9
Golf *David Arscott*	978-1-907184-75-8
The Olympics *David Arscott*	978-1-907184-78-9
The World Cup *David Arscott*	978-1-907184-38-3

Royalty

Kings & Queens of Great Britain *Antony Mason*	978-1-906714-77-2
Royal Weddings *Fiona Macdonald*	978-1-907184-84-0
The Tudors *Jim Pipe*	978-1-907184-58-1
Queen Elizabeth II Diamond Jubilee: 60 Years a Queen *David Arscott*	978-1-908177-50-6

Natural history

Cats *Fiona Macdonald*	978-1-908973-34-4
Dogs *Fiona Macdonald*	978-1-908973-35-1
Global Warming *Ian Graham*	978-1-907184-51-2

Ancient and medieval history

Ancient Egypt: Mummy Myth and Magic *Jim Pipe*	978-1-906714-92-5
Castles *Jacqueline Morley*	978-1-907184-48-2

Folklore and traditions

Christmas *Fiona Macdonald*	978-1-907184-50-5
Vampires *Fiona Macdonald*	978-1-907184-39-0

Myths and legends

Heroes, Gods and Monsters of Celtic Mythology *Fiona Macdonald*	978-1-905638-97-0

This is Volume 41 of The Cherished Library. A list of authors and their works in this series will be found on the preceding pages. The publishers will be pleased to send freely to all applicants an illustrated catalogue of the Library and our many other publications.

Book House
25 Marlborough Place
Brighton
BN1 1UB

www.salariya.com

Some reviews of other volumes in this series

Queen Elizabeth II Diamond Jubilee by David Arscott

'David Arscott's enjoyable quirky, irreverent style comes across in this entertaining fact-filled volume.'

David Ogilvy

Charles Dickens by Fiona Macdonald

'A really entertaining little book full of information, quotations and drawings. Easy to dip into and small enough to read while travelling.'

Tick Tock